The Story of Majorca and Minorca

Sir Clements R. Markham

Alpha Editions

This edition published in 2024

ISBN : 9789362922823

Design and Setting By
Alpha Editions
www.alphaedis.com
Email - info@alphaedis.com

As per information held with us this book is in Public Domain.
This book is a reproduction of an important historical work. Alpha Editions uses the best technology to reproduce historical work in the same manner it was first published to preserve its original nature. Any marks or number seen are left intentionally to preserve its true form.

Contents

PREFACE ....- 1 -

CHAPTER I Of King Jayme I. of Aragon and how he resolved to conquer Majorca and drive out the Moors..- 2 -

CHAPTER II Tells how King Jayme won a victory over the Moors of Majorca; and gives some account of the Moorish capital ....- 8 -

CHAPTER III Tells how En Jayme besieged and took the capital, conquered the whole island, and became the first Christian King of Majorca ....- 12 -

CHAPTER IV King Jayme's last visits—Settlement of the island—Acts and death of Jayme I., first King of Majorca...................................- 18 -

CHAPTER V Tells how the King of Aragon took up Conradin's glove; how the Pope's curses went home to roost; and how En Pedro kept his tryst ....- 24 -

CHAPTER VI Tells how the Queen of Aragon went to Sicily with her sons, how Admiral Lauria won new victories, and how more of the Pope's curses went home to roost ....- 33 -

CHAPTER VII Tells how young Federigo held Sicily against all odds, how the Catalan Company went to the east, and how Jayme of Majorca was restored to his island home...................................- 41 -

CHAPTER VIII Tells how King Jayme II. at last reigned in peace, and how his page Raimondo Lulio attained the crown of martyrdom..- 46 -

CHAPTER IX The career of Prince Fernando of Majorca; and tells how the orphan was taken home to its grandmother ....- 52 -

CHAPTER X King Sancho of Majorca.................................- 59 -

CHAPTER XI King Jayme III. of Majorca ....- 61 -

CHAPTER XII Relates the adventures of Jayme and Isabel, describes the memorial chair, and records the end of the Majorcan dynasty ....- 65 -

CHAPTER XIII Relates the story, so far as it concerns Majorca, of the last Kings of Aragon ....- 69 -

CHAPTER XIV The Majorcans as navigators .... -73 -

CHAPTER XV The Comunidades ....- 77 -

CHAPTER XVI The Majorcan historians—War of succession—Families ennobled—Cotoners—Raxa and Cardinal Despuig—Country houses ....- 81 -

CHAPTER XVII The Marquis of Romana and the patriot Jovellanos. ....- 86 -

CHAPTER XVIII Conclusion ....- 91 -

PART II Minorca...- 95 -

CHAPTER I Minorca—Its prehistoric remains—Mago the Carthaginian—Successive occupations .... -97 -

CHAPTER II Conquest of Minorca by Alfonso III.—The Barbary pirates............................- 101 -

CHAPTER III British occupation of Minorca..- 106 -

CHAPTER IV Minorca as a base ....- 111 -

CHAPTER V Minorca under British rule ....- 115 -

CHAPTER VI Minorca twice lost..- 119 -
CHAPTER VII The third occupation of
Minorca—Loss of British rule..- 123 -

PREFACE

The story of the Islands of Majorca and Minorca has never been told in our language in a condensed form, although the interest is great from an historical point of view, and the materials sufficient, though not perhaps abundant. It is so closely connected with the history of Aragon and the recovery of the Sicilies from the intruding Angevins that the two cannot be altogether separated. The most that can be done is, as far as practicable, to treat the Aragonese and Sicilian events from a Majorcan point of view. This has been attempted. The stirring events of the conquest of Majorca by Jayme I., the latter part of the reign of his son, and the reigns of Sancho and Jayme III., as well as the adventures and death of Jayme IV., the last of his race, all belong strictly to Majorcan history, as do the chapters on Balearic navigators and the revolt of the 'Comunidades.' The story fills a vi gap in the history of Mediterranean countries which may not be altogether unacceptable to students. This has been one object of the writer.

Another object has been to supply more detailed information respecting the events of former times in the islands, for the use of the considerable number of visitors who resort to them. The interest of the scenery and of many localities cannot fail to be much increased by a detailed knowledge of the historical associations connected with them.

My principal authorities have been the autobiography of Jayme I., the Chronicle of Muntaner, Desclot, Zurita, and the histories of Dameto and Mut, edited by Bover. My thanks are due for much courtesy and assistance from the Count of Montenegro, H.M. Consul Don Bartolomè Bosch y Cerda, and Señor Albareda of the Grand Hotel at Palma, and to Mr. Gilbert Ogilvy for having kindly made sketches for me of the memorial chair at Alfavia.

The story of Minorca necessarily embraces an account of the several British occupations, and of some of the operations of the British fleet with Minorca as a base.

      September 1908.

CHAPTER I
OF KING JAYME I. OF ARAGON AND HOW HE RESOLVED TO CONQUER MAJORCA AND DRIVE OUT THE MOORS

Majorca has a very interesting history under its Aragonese princes, and a history which has been well told by those princes themselves and by a loyal vassal who was a diligent seeker after truth. But to understand it we must turn first to the gorges of the Pyrenees and the ports of Catalonia.

By the middle of the eighth century the Moors had overcome Spain up to the Pyrenees, and established their rule and their religion in all parts of the country. But there they had to stop. They could not subdue the mountaineers of Asturias and the Basque provinces. Strong in their almost inaccessible valleys in the southern slopes of the Pyrenees, the ancestors of the nobles of Aragon also held their Moslem enemies at bay. Wild as those valleys were, they were beautiful and productive. Evergreen oaks clothed the lower slopes, succeeded by pine forests, and still higher up are the bushes and trees of box so characteristic of the Pyrenees. The mountaineers had their flocks and herds, crops of barley and oats, and abundance of timber. But there was a long struggle before them.

The little kingdom of Navarre was founded by Garcia Jimenes as early as 758, and Louis, the son of Charlemagne, drove the Moors out of Barcelona and established a Christian country there about fifty years afterwards. At length the kingdom of Aragon was founded by Ramiro I., a son of the King of Navarre, and Buesca was taken from the Moors and became the first capital of Aragon. Then the great Alonso, surnamed 'El Batallador,' having firmly established his power in the plains, drove the Moors out of Zaragoza in 1118, which was thenceforth the capital of Aragon.

The marriage of Petronilla, the heiress of Aragon, with Raymond Berenger, the Count of Barcelona, raised the kingdom to a position of importance among the nations of the Middle Ages. The Counts of Barcelona during three centuries had ruled over a maritime people of great energy. These rulers were, for the most part, capable men, whether in war or peace. The Berengers were great warriors. It is related that the first of the family passed his hand, covered with blood, down the face of his golden shield after a battle, and ever afterwards the arms of Barcelona, granted by the Emperor Charles the Bald in 873 and eventually adopted by Aragon, were *or four pales gules*.[1] The old arms of Aragon were a cross of St. George between four Moors' heads. They were quartered with those of Barcelona after the union; but latterly those of the Counts of Barcelona only were used. Sicily was *per saltire* the arms of Aragon (Barcelona) above and below, imperial eagles dexter and sinister. As rulers of a maritime and commercial people, the Counts were not found wanting. Count Raymond, called the 'Old,' gave the Catalans a code of laws and began the cathedral at Barcelona, and his successors fostered the rising importance of Catalan enterprise.

Aragon, like England, was a constitutional monarchy, with the 'Fueros de Sobrarbe' as its Magna Charta. The King could do nothing, in peace or war, without the counsel of the nobles, called 'Ricos Hombres,'[2] and there was a court of appeal in the 'Justicia Mayor.' The Parliament was composed of the 'Ricos Hombres' and the 'Syndicos' of the towns. Next in rank to the 'Ricos Hombres' were the 'Infançones,' equivalent to 'Hidalgos' in Castille. The prefix 'En' was used in Aragon as equivalent to 'Don' in Castille. The Catalan language, allied to the Provençal, was spoken by the people, and written by lawyers, chroniclers, and troubadours. It was extended to Valencia and the Balearic Isles, and claims great antiquity. It was the language of an enterprising commercial people, and was well adapted to be a vehicle for romantic and national songs.

The exact identity of duration of the two dynasties of Plantagenets and Aragonese sovereigns invites comparison. The heiress Petronilla was the contemporary of our Empress Maud; and Ferdinand, the last male of his race, was the contemporary of our last Plantagenet, Richard III. They were neighbours, the Pyrenees only separating Gascony of the Plantagenets from Aragon and Catalonia. They were cousins through Eleanor of Provence. They were more than cousins, for Raymond, the husband of Petronilla, chose our Henry II. for the guardian of his children, and the greatest of our kings, Edward I., was the trusted umpire selected by Pedro III. of Aragon, and the intended father-in-law of his son. Both families were composed of remarkable men, renowned for chivalry, bravery, and, in more instances than was the case in most dynasties, for wisdom as rulers.

Pedro II. of Aragon reigned from 1196 to 1213. He and his cousin En Nuño de Sans fought at the battle of Las Navas de Tolosa side by side with the kings of Castille and Navarre. It was the great conflict which finally settled the preponderance of Christians over Moors. After that famous victory the expulsion of the latter was only a question of time. Pedro married the heiress of Montpellier and became the Lord of that barony, as well as of Roussillon and Cerdaña. This brought him in contact with Simon de Montfort; and the King of Aragon appears to have made an agreement with Simon by which he gave his only son Jayme to be brought up at Carcassonne with a view to his eventual marriage with a daughter of De Montfort. Afterwards a war broke out between Aragon and Carcassonne, and Pedro was slain in a battle near the castle of Muret.

The heir of Aragon was at Carcassonne, in the power of his father's enemy, and was only six years of age. He was born on February 8, 1208. Simon de

Montfort at first refused to give him up; but, owing to the intervention of the Pope, he was restored to his subjects, and arrived at Montpellier in safety with his cousin Ramon Berenguer of Provence, who was the same age. This companion of Jayme was the future grandfather of Edward I. of England.

Jayme I. of Aragon, surnamed the Conqueror, was among the greatest sovereigns in an age of great sovereigns, the age of Edward I. of England, of St. Louis of France, of St. Fernando of Castille, of Frederick II. of Germany. Accepted by his Parliament and guarded by his nobles during his minority, Jayme entered upon his duties as ruler of a free people with every advantage. His person is described by Desclot. He was very tall—over six feet—with broad shoulders, small waist, and well-proportioned limbs. He had a fair rosy complexion, blue eyes, and auburn hair. He was strong and active, very expert in all exercises on foot or horseback, valiant and well-practised in arms. He was courteous and affable to all classes of people, and he was as merciful as he was brave. There is one charming incident which throws a very pleasant light on his character. It is related in his own journal. His tent had been pitched in one place for a considerable time, and when the camp was moving it was found that a swallow had built its nest between the tent-poles. The King ordered that the tent was to remain pitched and guarded until the young swallows could fly, saying that the mother-bird had put herself under his protection, and that he could not disappoint her.

Jayme, when a boy, was married to a princess of Castilla and had a son by her named Alonso, who died young. But the mother of his other children was Violante, daughter of King Andrew of Hungary and sister of St. Isabel.

The first great enterprise undertaken by King Jayme was the expulsion of the Moors from the Balearic Islands, which they had possessed for five hundred years.

Majorca, with its satellites Minorca and Iviça, forms a very fine possession. The largest of the islands, with its fifty miles of extent and area covering 1,300 square miles, is nearly square, with its two large bays of Palma and Alcudia on either side and a projection to the south-west; but the grace and beauty of its outline should have saved it from being called a 'quadrilateral trapezoid.' A fine range of mountains, mainly of Jurassic limestone (lias), occupies the western and northern sides of the island, with peaks rising to near 5,000 feet. The 'Puig Galatzo,' in sight from Palma, is 3,500, and the 'Puig Major,' farther north, 4,700 feet in height. The mountainous part contains lovely valleys, with much terrace-cultivation of oranges and olives, many flowering shrubs, and with the higher slopes clothed in forests of Aleppo pines. From this deep green vegetation perpendicular cliffs and peaks of white marble stand out against the deep blue sky. There are lower hills near the south coast, but the rest of the island is a most fertile *huerta* or garden, covered with almond and apricot trees, and crops or pasture beneath them. In the early spring the whole is one vast sea of almond-blossom. Ancient olive and carob trees take the place of almonds near the skirts of the mountains. On the northern side of the mountains, especially at Miramar, with the sea far below and the white peaks shooting up into the sky, the scene is a perfect dream of loveliness.

The Arab conquerors fully appreciated the beauty and advantages of Majorca, with its inheritance of Carthaginian and Roman traditions, ruins, and aqueducts. For does not the chronicler Ask-shakandi describe the island as 'one of the most fertile and best cultivated countries that God ever made, and the most abundant in provisions of all kinds'? while the poet Ibn-al-labneh tells us that to its capital 'the ringdove lent the prismatic colours of his collar, and the peacock his beautiful variegated plumage'!

It was in 716 that Abdallah, the son of Musa, overran the Balearic Islands, and they became part of the empire of the Beni Umiyyah. During this period they were fully occupied by Moors and Arabs. When the great Cordovan empire fell to pieces, a man of remarkable courage and ability was governor of the town of Denia, on the Valencian coast. This was Mujahid ibn Al Amíri, surnamed Abu-l-jayush, or the father of the army. He was a Cordovan, and a freed man of Abdu-r-rahman, son of the great conqueror Almanzor. Mujahid retained possession of Denia, and made himself Amir of the Balearic Islands in 1015. He was an undaunted warrior, an experienced sailor, and his large fleet dominated the eastern Mediterranean. His son Ali, surnamed Al Muhtadi, succeeded him in 1045, and was in close alliance with the Christian Count of Barcelona, Raymond Berenger I. A remarkable grant has been preserved by which Ali ordered that all the Christian clergy of Denia and the Balearic Islands were to be under the jurisdiction of the Bishop of Barcelona. It is a proof of the liberal and tolerant spirit which actuated the Spanish Muhammadan princes. Ali was dethroned by one of this officers named Mubashir, who reigned until 1114, and from that time, though the islanders throve and their capital was enriched, the rulers became aggressive and piratical. They were kept in check to some extent by the fleets of the republic of Pisa; but they made raids on the Catalonian coast, and even sacked Barcelona on one occasion and killed its Count. No Christian ship was safe, and at last the cup of their iniquity was full. King Jayme resolved that Majorca must be conquered and that the Moorish must be replaced by a Catalan population. It was time. The chroniclers call the Moor who was then ruling at Majorca 'Sheikh Bohibe,' but his real name appears to have been Abu Yahye ibn Ali Imran At-tinmeleli.

King Jayme, by keeping a journal, had an immense advantage over other sovereigns. His autobiography is deeply interesting in itself: its truthfulness is self-evident, and it checks and sometimes disproves the tales of careless chroniclers. It was printed at Valencia in 1474 in Catalan, the language in which it was written; was printed in Spanish for Philip II. in 1557; and Mr. Forster's English translation, edited by Don Pascual Gayangos, was published in 1883. Here we have a detailed narrative of the conquest of Majorca at first hand.

The young King was only in his twentieth year when the great enterprise was undertaken. He ruled over a free people, and it was necessary to call together the Ricos Hombres, the prelates, and the procurators of towns, and to submit his project for their approval. They assembled in the old palace of the Counts of Barcelona. Their assent was unanimous and enthusiastic. The Archbishop of Tarragona, too old to go himself, promised to equip one hundred knights and one thousand infantry. Then up rose En Berenguer de Palou, the Bishop of Barcelona, who was not to be outdone. He declared that he would go himself with 130 knights, one thousand soldiers, and a galley, and that he would not return until the conquest was complete. Other prelates—canons, abbots, and monks—followed these examples, down to the sacristan of Gerona, who promised to equip ten knights. The most able and experienced general among the nobles was the King's cousin En Nuño Sans, the Count of Roussillon, and he spoke in the names of the principal Ricos Hombres, who were En Guillem de Moncada, Viscount of Bearne by marriage, a very great vassal; Ponce Hugo, Count of Ampurias; Ramon de Moncada; Bernardo de Santa Eugenia de Torrella; Jofre, Viscount of Rocaberti; Hugo de Mataplana—all promising to equip knights and foot soldiers according to their means. The young son of a German count, named Carroz, and many other volunteers, also followed the King.

Ramon de Plegamans, a wealthy merchant of Barcelona, contracted to supply arms, siege equipage, and provisions; and the thoroughness with which this was done impresses the reader, more than the numbers of troops, with the wealth and resources of the great Catalonian seaport. As many as 143 vessels were assembled, including 25 full-sized ships, 18 undecked 'taridas,' and 100 flat-bottomed boats. The largest ship came from Narbonne, and had three decks. The army consisted of 15,000 infantry and 1,500 cavalry. All the latest machines for hurling stones and protecting the besiegers were provided by the enterprising Plegamans.

The vessels were assembled at the small ports of Salou and Cambrils, near Tarragona, and the expedition sailed on September 1, 1229. The King's orders were that the ship of Captain Nicolas Bonet, with En Guillermo de Moncada on board, should lead, and that young Carroz should command the rear ship. The King was in a galley belonging to Montpellier, his birthplace. There was a light wind from the shore, but before evening it began to blow hard from the south-west, with a very heavy sea. The ships were close-hauled, and making such bad weather that the pilot wanted to put back. The King would not hear of it. Towards sunset of the following day the land was in sight, and next morning the fleet was off Pollenza, the north-east extreme of Majorca. But suddenly a strong 'Provençal' wind sprang up, and the ships were in great danger of being driven on shore. By advice of an experienced sailor, they stood along the north-west coast of the island until the south-west extremity was reached at a place called Palomera. The King's galley arrived first, and was followed by the rest of the fleet, not one being missing. There was a consultation with En Nuño and the Moncadas, when it was agreed that the galleys should examine the south-west coast for a good place to land, while the rest of the fleet remained at anchor. The King landed on a rock between the island of Dragonera and the main, called Pantaleu, where he passed the following Sunday. The Moors had discovered the hostile fleet, and lined the shore with a strong force of horse and foot.

At midnight the fleet was got under way, with all lights out, and in profound silence. The main portion anchored in the bay of Santa Ponza, and the rest in a neighbouring roadstead called Porrasa. Thence the coast runs south to Cape Calafiguera, and sweeps round the bay of Palma. Here King Jayme landed with his army.

CHAPTER II
TELLS HOW KING JAYME WON A VICTORY OVER THE MOORS OF MAJORCA; AND GIVES SOME ACCOUNT OF THE MOORISH CAPITAL

The little bay of Santa Ponza was alive with boats from the ships, pulling to the shore. The first to land was a young Catalan ensign named Bernardo de Riudemeya, who waved his pennon as a sign for the others to follow him. As a reward the King granted him the estate of Santa Ponza in fee-simple. He was followed by 700 men and the chief officers, including En Nuño, En Ramon de Moncada, En Bernardo de Santa Eugenia de Torrella, Bernardo de Champans, the Master of the Temple, and his knights, making about 150 horse. A reconnaissance by Ramon de Moncada found an advanced guard of Moors about a mile away, which was attacked and put to flight. When the King landed, he heard that this encounter was proceeding, so he galloped off to the scene of action with forty attendant knights. Seeing a body of 400 Moorish infantry on a spur of the hills, he attacked them furiously, put them to flight, and returned well pleased. He found his nobles in some alarm for his safety, and he was seriously taken to task for running such risks when so much depended on his life. Guillem de Moncada told him that he ought to recollect that the lives of all of them depended upon his safety.

The rest of the cavalry had arrived in the rear squadron and had been landed at Porrasa, where it was ascertained that the Moorish Amír with a large army was at Porto Pi, a small harbour between Porrasa and the capital of the island. This news was brought to the King at midnight, and he called a council of war, when it was determined to give the troops a good night's rest before the expected battle. At dawn Jayme and his nobles heard Mass, and a sermon was preached by the Bishop of Barcelona. All prayed fervently, and were resolved upon victory. The King and most of his friends had received the Sacrament before starting, at Salou; but En Guillem de Moncada had delayed until this moment, desiring to do so on the very eve of battle.

Then the Moncadas, Mataplana, and some other knights, with 5,000 men, commenced a rapid advance against the enemy, apparently without orders. The Count of Ampurias followed with his men. A desperate fight was commenced, the Moors being in overwhelming numbers. Seeing the danger, the King galloped forward with a single knight, named Rocafort, in hopes of being in time to make the vanguard halt until the rest of the army could come up. He sent back Rocafort, when he heard the clang of arms;

with an urgent message to En Nuño to bring up supports, as the vanguard was surrounded. Jayme was in extreme anxiety. He was heard to say to himself, 'En Nuño delays much. The Holy Virgin preserve us!' An experienced veteran, En Nuño saw that all was in order before he led the main body of the army into battle.

In about an hour En Nuño came to where the King was, who had galloped forward without arming himself. Bertran de Naya, one of his servants, brought the royal accoutrements, and Jayme put on his quilted coat, his coat of mail, and iron cap in the field. He told the general that the vanguard was engaged with the whole force of the enemy, and a rapid advance was made to the scene of action. Here the King met a knight named En Guillem de Mediona, who had great fame as a jouster in tournaments. He was coming out of the battle. He said he had been wounded by a stone on the lip. In a severe tone, King Jayme said that it was not seemly to retire owing to so slight a hurt. Mediona blushed with shame, turned his horse's head and galloped into the thick of the fight, where he found a soldier's death.

The King had been delayed by the necessity of putting on his armour. He then advanced up a hill which to this day is called 'El Collado del Rey,' attended by only twelve soldiers. On reaching the summit he found En Nuño marshalling his forces for the battle, and close at hand the vast army of the Moors, with the Amír's red-and-white banner, the staff surmounted by a human head. The King, full of martial ardour, wanted to charge at once, but was restrained by En Nuño. Both armies joined battle, and, after a long contested engagement, the Moors broke and fled. The rout was so complete that the Amír took refuge in the mountains instead of returning to his capital. The Aragonese troops were too tired to continue the pursuit, and soon very sad news was brought respecting the fate of the vanguard.

The Bishop of Barcelona had to announce to the King that both En Guillem de Moncada, Viscount of Bearne, and En Ramon Moncada were slain, and that nearly all their men were cut to pieces before the main body of the army arrived on the field. Hugo de Mataplana was also among the slain. Young Jayme burst into tears at the loss of so many dear friends and comrades. The whole army mourned with their King. But they were now in sight of the beautiful city, the capture of which would be the crown of their enterprise. The King was dead tired and nearly famished, for he had eaten nothing all day. Going down a mountain spur, in company with En Nuño, they came upon a tent pitched under the pine-trees, amidst brushwood consisting of tree heaths, lentisco, and wild lavender. There was the smell of a good dinner in preparation, and here the tired warriors appeased their hunger, their host being En Oliver de Termens, a gallant Frenchman of Roussillon. When the King rose from an excellent meal he said, 'Ben dinat,' which in Catalan means 'well dined.' The spot retains the name to this day.

Long the property of the Caro family, from which sprang that gallant Marquis de la Romana who brought the Spanish troops from Denmark to join in the War of Independence, the historical spot has been much changed in recent times. A stately castle with towers at the angles, surrounded by gardens and orange-groves, has taken the place of En Oliver's tent where the young King dined so well 680 years ago. It was built in recent years by the Hungarian Marquesa de la Romana, who afterwards sold it. The castle of Bendinat is now owned by the Marquis de la Torre.

The interment of the great lords who were slain in the vanguard was conducted with all the pomp that was possible. A stone pillar surmounted by an iron cross now marks the spot. On one side is the date, September 12, 1229; on another the date of erection, 1884; and on a third the arms of Barcelona impaling those of Moncada (*gules, four bezants in pale*). It is on the left-hand side of the road, just halfway between Palma and Andraix, under the shade of a fine old pine-tree.

The scene of these military operations is exceedingly beautiful. The spurs from the main chain of mountains by the western sea are well covered with pine and ilex forests, and rise one behind the other. From them spurs covered with olives and carob-trees and an undergrowth of bright green crops and grass slope down to the sea. Some of the spurs form a lower chain, called the Sierra de Burguesa, overlooking Porto Pi and the capital.

The exposed bay of Palma, fifteen miles across, has the little harbour of Porto Pi on the west side, and the city of Mallorca, afterwards called Palma, in its centre. In Moorish times the city was an important commercial port, with a great fleet of piratical galleys. It had a strong wall and ditch, and eight gates. The bed of a mountain torrent formed the moat on the west side. On the sea-face there were three gates: one leading to the mole, called 'the Gate of Chains'; another to the west, called *Balbelet*, leading from the *Dar-as-Sanâá* or arsenal, corrupted by the Catalans into '*Atarazana*.' In the east of the sea-wall was the *Hicolbelet*. On the right of the Gate of Chains, within the walls, stood the Moorish palace, which appears to have been a small town in itself, called *El Medînah*, and by the Spaniards to this day *Almudaina*. On the east side there was a gate near the south-east angle, since closed up. Near the north-east angle was the *Belalcofol*, called by the Spaniards '*Pintada*.' On the north side was the *Barbolet*, now the *Puerto de Jesus*. The Moors had two gates on the side of the torrent, facing west, the *Belalbelet*, since closed, and the gate of Porto Pi, now called *Catalina*. Altogether there seem to have been eight gates in the Moorish walls. Besides the *Almudaina* there was a strong castle near the south-east angle of the town, which was given to the Knights Templars, and near the centre stood the chief mosque. Of other public buildings in Moorish times there is no notice.

The city of the Moors, owing to its wealth and importance, must have contained many fine and richly furnished houses; but such an active energetic people as the Catalans very soon replaced them with churches, convents, and houses in their own style, and there is but one vestige left. Walking down a street at the back of the cathedral, called 'Serra,' to the sea-face, the shrubs and flowers of a garden show themselves over a high wall. A flight of steps leads to the garden, and in one corner an archway opens on the ruins of a Moorish bath, though nothing is left but the bare brickwork. There is a dome supported by twelve pillars, with capitals apparently from the ruins of a Roman temple, the pillars about eight feet high, and the conventional leaf capitals not exactly fitting them. Round the dome there is a vaulted passage, with recesses for piping. This is all that remains to bear witness of the Moorish palaces and houses, with their wealth of arabesque work and bright colouring, their marble pillars and pavements, their cool gardens and fountains and luxurious baths. All is now a dream of the long-buried past.

CHAPTER III
TELLS HOW EN JAYME BESIEGED AND TOOK THE CAPITAL, CONQUERED THE WHOLE ISLAND, AND BECAME THE FIRST CHRISTIAN KING OF MAJORCA

The rout of the Moorish army removed any obstacle to the commencement of the siege of the capital. The western side of the walls faced the Catalans as they approached from the hills above Porto Pi, but it was defended by a torrent-bed. After a careful reconnaissance, it was resolved to deliver the main attack on the north-east side, at the *Belalcofol* gate, called by the Spaniards '*Pintada*.' Accordingly the King formed his camp facing this gate and about a mile distant, at a place still called 'El Real,' or 'the camp.' It was surrounded by a ditch and strong palisades, for it appears that the infantry went to sleep on board the ships every night, leaving only the knights and artillery in the camp.

Mallorca was very strongly fortified, the walls being of great thickness, with towers at intervals. It was therefore determined to batter down the walls and make a breach with the artillery so efficiently provided by the zealous contractor, Ramon de Plegamans. The King mentions four kinds of artillery for hurling rocks against the walls, which he calls *trebuchets* or catapults, *almajanachs*, *algarradas*, and *fonebols*, the latter being the stone balls themselves, not the machines. These were the latest things in siege artillery; but the King was not content with them and ordered a still larger machine to be constructed out of the yards and masts of the ships, as well as *mantellos* for the protection of the workmen. The Moors had similar artillery within the walls, one of their machines with such a range as to reach the Christian camp.

The zealous ardour of the Catalan army was stimulated and kept alive not only by the example of the young King, but also by the fiery eloquence of a friar preacher named Miguel Fabra. All worked alike, from the King himself to the meanest labourer. But although a continual watch was kept round the walls, the Amír succeeded one dark night in effecting an entrance with a number of his followers.

The Moors were not without supporters outside the town, who were ready to harass the Christians. One of the principal Moslem chiefs in the mountains was Fatih-billah ('Conqueror by the grace of God'), a word corrupted by the Spaniards into 'Infantilla.' About two Spanish leagues[3] from the town there was an abundant spring, with a channel leading from it, bearing a copious supply of good water. The Christian camp was pitched by the side of this channel. The place where the spring rises is called Canet, near the foot of the mountains. The actual spring was on a wooded hill sloping down to a beautiful little valley, with the main range of the mountains on the other side. Fatih-billah hoped to do irreparable injury to the besiegers by cutting off their water-supply. So one night he went to Canet with 500 footmen and 100 horse, occupied the hill where the spring rises, and began to turn the water into another channel. Directly this was known at the camp, the King despatched a much larger force under En Nuño and Torrella, which surprised the Moors at their work. There was a desperate encounter on the hillside; Fatih-billah was killed, his men were cut to pieces, and the spring remained in possession of the Catalans. How changed is now the scene! The large country house of the descendants of Torrella dominates the valley of Canet, with its beautiful gardens and woods of fir-trees and heath beyond. The hillside is terraced for olive-trees and carobs; and a few years ago a stalactite cave was discovered there, several hundred yards in length, the entrance to which is close to the spot where the battle between En Nuño and Fatih-billah must have been fought. The cave was then unknown. It would easily have held the whole of the Moorish force, and the Catalans would have been unaware of their proximity. The discovery appears to have been made owing to a perforation in the roof of the cave which made a hole in a field above.

This was the last attempt to molest the besiegers from outside, or by sallies in force. Nevertheless the King caused a tower called 'El Torre de las Lanoveras,' between the capital and Porto Pi, to be fortified, and a guard to be stationed there, so as to keep a close watch on the movements of the enemy.

The Catalans received important assistance from the friendship of a very influential Moor named Benahabet, who was anxious to be on the winning side. He was highly connected, was Governor of Pollenza and Inca, and owner of the beautiful country seat of Alfavia. He sent a messenger declaring that he would place a third of the island in the power of King Jayme. Soon afterwards he came himself with a very large supply of fresh provisions, and was received into the King's grace. The supply was renewed every week. Benahabet suggested that, as the towns in his jurisdiction had submitted, two principal Christian officers should be sent to bear rule over them and to administer justice. Two such officers—one a native of Barcelona, the other of Montpellier were appointed with the title of 'Baile,' or Judge.

The besiegers continued to work hard at the approaches and mines, both sides receiving much injury from the stone-hurling artillery. Seeing the rapid progress of the Christians, the Amír made a request that the King would send some one to treat with him. En Nuño went, with a dozen attendant knights and an interpreter. The Amír offered to pay all the expenses of the expedition if the Christians would depart; but the King positively refused to consider any such terms. The Amír then prayed for a second interview, and pitched a sumptuously furnished tent near Porto Pi. Hostilities were suspended, and En Nuño came again. The Amír made a dissertation on the impossibility of taking so strong a place, and merely offered the same terms. When this was again refused, he offered five besants for each man, woman, and child, and to surrender the town, if he was allowed a number of ships sufficient to take all his people to Barbary. En Nuño came back with this offer, but the relations and friends of the Moncadas insisted that the place should be taken without any treaty or agreement. At first En Jayme was inclined to accept the Moor's offer, but eventually he gave way to the strong feeling of his nobles, and all negotiations were broken off.

As soon as he found that there was no hope from negotiation, the Amír resolved upon a desperate defence. He addressed his people, urging them to defend their religion, their liberty, and their homes to the death. He met with a determined response, and the resistance became more fierce and desperate than ever. The Count of Ampurias conducted the mining operations, and eventually at least forty yards of the wall fell in. The breach was defended with such furious valour that the besiegers were forced to retire, while the Moors hastily built up another wall. A few days afterwards, on the Saturday after St. Andrew's,[4] another piece of the wall, with a tower, fell in heaps. With the accord of the army, the King then resolved to deliver the assault on the following Sunday morning. Still the resistance was so resolute, the furious struggles for positions so prolonged, that it was the last day of December before the general assault could be given.

At dawn the troops heard Mass and received the Sacrament. The King made a speech to animate the men, with whom he promised to conquer or die. They advanced to the ruined walls, where the *'Puerta Pintada'* stood, and 300 footmen rushed over the breach, followed by cavalry. The Moorish Amír was at the head of his bravest warriors, and soon a desperate battle was raging in the street now called 'San Miguel.' Mounted on a white horse, and armed at all points, the gallant Moor courted death, and kept shouting to his men, 'Stand firm! Stand firm!' The brave defenders died in heaps where they stood, but the impulse of the Catalans was irresistible, and they reached the front of the chief mosque, leaving heaps of dead behind them.

This mosque was turned into the first Christian place of worship, and is now the church of San Miguel. The figure-head of the King's galley was a Virgin and Child. It was placed in the church of San Miguel, where it remains to this day.

Here there was a pause. The Moors still fought hard to prevent a further advance into their city, while stones and timber were hurled upon the assailants by women and children on the roofs. So long as their Amír led them the Moors continued the struggle, but at last he retired in despair.

Then the inhabitants began to pour out of the gates now called Jesus and Catalina, and fled towards the mountains. The dead could be counted by thousands. The King placed himself at the head of his troops and led them through the town until he reached the 'Almudaina' palace on the sea-face. Those within it surrendered on condition that their lives were spared.

The house in which his brave antagonist the Amír Abu Yahye had taken refuge was pointed out to King Jayme. He went there, accompanied by his cousin En Nuño. When he entered the room, the Amír, who was in a white burnous and quilted coat, stood up and tendered his submission. The King received it with courtesy, promised the Amír his life, and treated him with consideration, giving him in charge to two of his nobles. En Jayme found the Amír's son, a boy aged about fourteen, in the 'Almudaina.' He adopted the young Moorish prince, converted him, and eventually granted him a considerable estate in Aragon, where he married the fair Eva de Roldan and became Baron of Hillueca and Gotor.

Having placed a strong guard over the treasury in the 'Almudaina,' the King, quite worn out by the fatigue of so many days of anxiety and fighting, retired to rest in the Moorish palace. On the following morning the city was given up to sack, and the spoils were enormous, consisting of great quantities of gold and silver in many shapes, rich clothing, arms, horses, and a thousand other forms of riches. The soldiers were well repaid for their labours. The sacking of the town was allowed to proceed for eight days continuously. As many as 180 Christian captives were found and liberated. Efforts were then made to bury the dead, but they were ineffectual, and a terrible pestilence broke out. One of the first victims was the Count of Ampurias; many other leading nobles perished, and great ravages were made among the soldiers before the pestilence subsided.

The Catalan force had been much reduced by losses during the siege, by some having returned home, and by the pestilence, and no reinforcements had arrived. Yet the King insisted upon attacking a large body of Moors who had taken refuge in the mountains. Fortunately, the impregnable castle of Alaro, which he left on his right as he advanced, had been secured by his ally Benahabet, and was not in the hands of the Moors. The King led his men to the skirts of the mountains, at a place called Buñola, where he appears to have sustained a serious reverse. The Catalans fed before the mountaineers, and never stopped until they reached Benahabet's town of Inca, near the centre of the island. The King followed the fugitives with only forty attendant knights, and sternly upbraided them for their cowardice. He then returned to Palma with his beaten troops.

Soon afterwards a welcome reinforcement arrived, which, however, only consisted of fifteen well-armed knights. But their leader was a man of exceptional importance. Hugo de Folch Alguer was Master of the Knights of St. John of Jerusalem in Aragon and Catalonia, and was a veteran for whom the King had a great regard. His request for a grant of land for his Order was opposed at first by the nobles who had borne the heat and burden of the day. It speaks much for the tact and conciliatory skill of the young King that he eventually succeeded in making the grant to the Master with the consent and approval of all concerned in the division of the land.

En Jayme then resolved to lead an expedition against the Moors who had taken refuge in the hills towards the south-east angle of the island. Accompanied by En Nuño, the Bishop of Barcelona, and the Master of the Hospitallers, the King advanced to the site of Manacor, now the centre of a vine-growing district. Here the news came that many Moors were concealed, with their riches, in almost inaccessible caves near the south coast.

On the coast near Manacor is the *Cueva del Drach*, one of the largest stalactite caves in Europe, with several subsidiary caves and an underground lake, over which the myriads of stalactites present a fairy-like scene. Farther to the eastward the caves of Arta are of still greater extent, nearly 300 yards long, in three vast vaulted halls, roofed by magnificent stalactites, some of them assuming marvellous shapes. The approach to the entrance, where there is a splendid view over the sea, has now been made easy enough. In the thirteenth century it was extremely difficult and perilous. The young King led an assault on the caves of Arta, but, unable to face the hail storm of missiles on so narrow and dangerous a path, his men were repulsed. A retreat was unavoidable, and En Jayme went to dinner. The Master of St. John, with his knights, then endeavoured to set fire to some huts built round the entrance of the caves. The plan was to send two knights on to the heights above the entrance, whence they were to shower down darts made with artificial fire, so as to burn the huts and fill the cave with suffocating smoke. Two brothers named Antonio and Perote Moix volunteered for this dangerous service. The plan was successful, and the Moors, from fear of suffocation, offered to surrender if no succour reached them in eight days. Meanwhile the Catalans were suffering from want of provisions. The King himself, with En Nuño and a hundred followers, only had seven loaves of bread amongst them for a whole day. The rest of the army fed on corn stored in the farms. The young son of Ramon de Moncada, who secured the bread, received for his arms *'on a field gules seven loaves or.'*

On Palm Sunday, 1230, the Moorish fugitives in the various caves surrendered, to the number of 1,500 men, women, and children, with an immense quantity of wheat and barley, cows and sheep, and jewels of gold and silver. En Jayme returned in triumph to Palma, where his satisfaction was increased by the arrival of a large reinforcement. Soon afterwards some of the Moors in the western mountains submitted to the conqueror.

The King busied himself with the political settlement of the land, dividing the estates among his nobles and knights, and granting very extensive privileges to the Catalan settlers. He then resolved to return to his Continental dominions. En Bernardo de Santa Eugenia, Lord of Torrella, was appointed the first Governor and Captain-General of the kingdom of Majorca. His descendants still enjoy the *quinta* of Canet and other estates granted to him. His brother was the first Bishop. The Moorish prisoners were made to labour on the public works. Those who had submitted voluntarily were allowed to retain houses and lands, paying rent and cultivating the ground. Some became Christians. Soon many settlers arrived with their wives, while many wives of the soldiers joined their husbands.

At length the day came for the King to depart. He was much beloved, and there was general mourning. He made a farewell speech, and the knights who had gone through so many dangers and hardships with him were affected to tears. With only two galleys King Jayme embarked at the port of Palomera on October 28, 1230, and landed near Tarragona. He was received with great rejoicings by all classes of the people.

CHAPTER IV
KING JAYME'S LAST VISITS—SETTLEMENT OF THE ISLAND—ACTS AND DEATH OF JAYME I., FIRST KING OF MAJORCA

The settlement of the country was continued under Bernardo de Torrella, though there were still about two thousand Moors holding out in the mountains under a chief called by the Spaniards Xoarp. Soon alarming news arrived that the King of Tunis was preparing to reconquer Mallorca with a large army, and that he had collected a great number of ships to transport it. The tidings were sent to the King, and were confirmed by Plegamans, who was a newsagent as well as a contractor. En Jayme resolved to go in person to defend his island, in spite of the remonstrances of many of his councillors, who deprecated his exposure to so many dangers. The old Archbishop of Tarragona went so far as to try and hold him round the waist when he was getting into the boat at Salou.

This time the King brought with him a cousin to be Viceroy of Mallorca, in the person of the Infante Pedro of Portugal. This prince's mother was Aldonza, sister of Alonso II. of Aragon and wife of Sancho, King of Portugal; so that Pedro was a first cousin of King Jayme's father—the same relation as En Nuño. He married the Countess of Urgel, the greatest heiress in Aragon, and acquired a position of importance in the country. The Countess had died without children, and Pedro received Mallorca on condition that he surrendered all his rights in the county of Urgel. He seems to have been a weak man, fond of his ease, and all real power remained with Torrella and others trusted by the King.

En Jayme, accompanied by En Nuño and the Portuguese prince, sailed from Salou, and in two days his little fleet was anchored in the port of Soller, where the joyful news was received that the King of Tunis had abandoned his intended invasion, at all events for that year. The port of Soller is on the north side of the island, about two miles from the town, which is in the midst of a lovely valley surrounded by magnificent mountain peaks. Rich in the products of its harvests, Soller was even then a place of trade, and En Jayme found a Genoese vessel loading in its port. The King must have been struck by the wonderful beauty of this side of his island, which he had not seen before. Suliar (Soller) in Arabic means a shell, like the golden shell at Palermo. It is now, and probably was then, golden with orange and lemon gardens; the higher slopes of the mountains covered with pine and carob trees, and the grand peaks raising their heads into the sky. The loftiest peak in the island, 'Puig Mayor d'en Torrello' (4,700 feet) is not in sight, being concealed by the second highest, the 'Puig de Massonella' (4,400 feet), on which the King probably saw patches of snow. To the north-east is a striking peak, called 'Puig de L'Ofre' (3,500 feet), and to the south the 'Teix' of Valdemosa (3,400 feet). In the division the King gave two-thirds of the Soller valley to the Count of Ampudia, and one-third to Gaston de Moncada, whose father was slain in the battle of Santa Ponza. In riding from Soller to Palma King Jayme had to cross a mountain saddle 2,000 feet high, whence he had glorious views of the Soller valley on one side, and of the fertile 'garden' of Palma on the other. At the end of the descent is the estate of Alfavia, the enchanting country seat of Jayme's Moorish ally, Benahabet. The estate had been granted to En Nuño, but the Moorish owners were allowed to retain it on paying a quit-rent. Here the King probably rested before riding across the '*huerta*,' or garden, to Palma, where he was received with transports of joy by the people.

The King was unable to remain long away from his Continental dominions. He left the Infante Pedro of Portugal as Viceroy, Bernardo de Torrella and a knight named Pedro Maza being the real governors.

There were still over two thousand insurgent Moors in the recesses of the mountains, and their leader refused to surrender to anyone but the King himself. On this being represented to En Jayme, he resolved to pay a third visit to his island kingdom, and sailed from Salou with three galleys in May 1232. He landed at Porto Pi, and was joyfully received by his loyal subjects, who were able to show him great progress in the public works at Palma. The cathedral had been traced out on a site facing the sea, close to the east wall of the Almudaina, and the royal chapel, which was to be the apse containing the high altar, was actually finished. Between the long lancet windows there are marble statues of saints and angels on corbels and under richly carved canopies, placed there at the cost of the Oleza family. This chapel and one on either side were to form the eastern ends of the nave and two aisles, not yet commenced. The King was much pleased at the progress that had been made.

The time had now come for the submission of the other Balearic islands; but first the King received the surrender of the Moorish mountain chief, he and his followers being allowed to retain their homes, paying rent to their overlords. A few obstinate fanatics refused the terms, and had to be starved out.

The Master of the Templars in Majorca, Friar Ramon Serra, was the first to suggest to the King that his galleys should be sent to Minorca, demanding immediate submission and threatening that the King would himself come with a large army to punish any disobedience. The three knights, Torrella, Maza, and Serra himself, were accordingly ordered to proceed to Minorca with an interpreter, and the King's demand written in Arabic. The Moorish Alcaide and headmen of the town received the knights with much respect.

The letter was read to them, and they asked for time to deliberate. This was granted. On that very evening the King, with only six knights, was stationed on Cape Pera, the eastern extreme of the island of Majorca, near Arta, with Minorca clearly in sight. As soon as the sun set they fired some immense piles of *lentisco* bushes, to make the Minorcans believe that a great army was encamped there. When the chief men of Minorca saw the fires, they hurried to the Catalan knights to inquire what they were. 'It is the great army,' they were told, 'that will come directly the King hears of a refusal of his demands.' Next day they submitted, surrendered all their strong places, and declared that they trusted in the clemency of the King. Meanwhile En Jayme remained on the Cape of Pera, continuing the stratagem of the bonfires for four days, when the news of the submission of Minorca without bloodshed was brought and gave him great satisfaction. Iviza and Formentera submitted in the following year.

The King was in Majorca during July and August 1232. He granted very liberal *Fueros* to the people and completed the settlement of the island. The final document in which the distribution of lands among the conquerors is recorded was signed on July 1, 1232. The lands were divided into *jovadas*, and these were subdivided into *cuarteradas*, a *cuarterada* being a certain portion of squared land, with each side forty *brazas* in length. A *braza* was the length of King Jayme's arms from finger-tips to finger-tips, and, as he was over six feet, this was a good fathom. The length of each side of a *cuarterada* was therefore eighty English yards. A *jovada* was originally the portion of land that a yoke of bullocks could plough in one day; but in the Majorca division it was counted at sixteen *cuarteradas*. The Arabic names were used, *rahal* being a house or property near a town; *alqueria* a farm, a word still in use; *beni* preceding a place-name meaning 'the house of.' As many as 573 *rahales* and *alquerias* were thus granted by the King, the grantees paying certain dues to the four great feudatories, En Nuño, Count of Roussillon, the Count of Ampurias, Gaston de Moncada, and the Bishop of Barcelona. But this only includes half the grants, the rest having been made by the great feudatories themselves to their own followers. Altogether upwards of fifteen hundred farms must have been distributed. There was also a division of the mills, and of the rights to running water. The number of farms gives an idea of the flourishing condition of the island in the time of the Moors. They were succeeded by an equally energetic and intelligent race of farmers and artisans.

The Knights Templars received the strong castle near the south-eastern angle of the city walls, afterwards called the Temple, and a great number of farms. The Knights Hospitallers also acquired very considerable landed property.

On a small island the population, under circumstances like the conquest of Mallorca, is soon changed. A great number of the Moors perished, many escaped to Muhammadan Spain or Africa, many were taken away by their new masters. There is certainly no trace of Moorish blood among the present inhabitants.

The government of Majorca, according to the *Fueros* of King Jayme I., granted in 1240, consisted of six persons, elected annually, called *Jurados*, who formed the municipal authority. The president, called *Jurado en cap*, belonged to the class of nobles; two were citizens liable for military service, two were of the merchant class, and one of the labouring class. Until 1447 the *Jurados* were co-opted, but afterwards a sort of ballot was adopted. There was a General Council of 143 deputies, the *Jurado en cap* presiding. The deputies consisted of a fixed number of representatives of the capital and other towns, and of knights, merchants, and artisans. There was one judge, called the *Bayle General*, until the institution of the Audiencia in 1576. This was a remarkably liberal constitution for the thirteenth century, and indicates the trust and reliance felt by King Jayme in the loyalty and good sense of his people. In this, as in other respects, we are reminded of our own Edward I., his parliaments and legislation.

The conquest of Majorca was a matter of the greatest importance to the island, but it was only a brief episode in the long reign of more than sixty years. En Jayme showed ceaseless activity in the work of government, consulting assemblies of his people, framing laws and granting privileges, and settling complicated disputes. Popular representation was strengthened under Jayme I. He sometimes met the Cortes of Aragon in the capital or one of the towns, and the Council of Catalonia separately; at other times the representatives, for special reasons, met in one assembly, usually at Monzon. In one case the meeting was called a parliament, in the other 'Cortes Generales.' Mr. Hallam, in his 'Middle Ages,' has given a good general account of the Aragonese Constitution. En Jayme frequently visited the whole of his dominions, and thus became intimately acquainted with his people and their needs. In 1238, nine years after the conquest of Majorca, King Jayme found it necessary, owing to the frequent and audacious inroads of the Moors, to undertake the conquest of the rich and important kingdom of Valencia. The capital city was taken at Michaelmas, and a Christian population substituted; but it was a much longer military operation to reduce the numerous strongholds up to the frontier of Murcia. The work was finally completed, and King Jayme, well named 'El Conquistador,' granted *Fueros* to his new kingdom of Valencia, and a representative assembly, or Cortes.

It now becomes necessary to allude to the King's children and family relations. By his wife Violante of Hungary Jayme I. had eight children. Pedro, his successor in Aragon, Catalonia, and Valencia, was born in 1243. In July 1262, at the age of nineteen, he was married to Constance, daughter of Manfred, King of Sicily, son of the Emperor Frederick II., by Beatrice, daughter of Amadeo, Count of Savoy. The marriage took place at Montpellier. The second son was Jayme, who was to succeed his father as King of Majorca, as well as to the possessions in the south of France. King Jayme married his second son to Esclaramunda, sister of the Count of Foix, the most powerful nobleman in Gascony. The third son, Fernando, did not turn out well. Of the daughters, Violante married Alonso X., King of Castille, in 1248; Isabel became the wife of King Philip III. (*le Hardi*) of France; and Constance of the Infante Don Manuel of Castille. Maria was a nun, and Leonor, the youngest, died in childhood.

The Infante Pedro of Portugal died childless in 1244, and was buried in the cathedral at Palma. En Nuño, the King's cousin and most able general, also dying childless, left all his vast possessions to the master he had served so long and so well. He was Count of Roussillon, Cerdaña, and Conflent.

After the marriages of his children, the last great enterprise of En Jayme was undertaken at the earnest request of his son-in-law, Alonso X. of Castille. This was the conquest of the Muhammadan kingdom of Murcia, in which his son Pedro took a prominent part. The campaign was a complete success, and King Jayme honourably handed over to Alonso X. the prize he had won at great cost and no little trouble. He also made some liberal grants in the south of Valencia to his other son-in-law, the Infante Manuel.

Jayme was happy in his two sons Pedro and Jayme, both brave, accomplished, and dutiful. He determined to provide for both. Pedro was to succeed his father as King of Aragon, King of Valencia, and Count of Barcelona. He thus, by the addition of Valencia, gave to his heir far more extensive dominions than he had himself inherited. To his second son, Jayme, he gave the kingdom of Majorca, the counties of Roussillon, Cerdaña, and Conflent in the Pyrenees, inherited from En Nuño, and the barony of Montpellier, the inheritance of his mother. He declared his resolution to make this division on January 19, 1248, and his act was recognised and confirmed by the Cortes in 1251, and again in 1262. Pedro could have no cause for complaint, because he succeeded to all that his father had inherited and a great deal more. The division was confirmed many years before the death of King Jayme, so that both his sons had ample time to become reconciled to an arrangement which was perfectly fair and just in itself. Young Jayme, indeed, assumed his position in Majorca as heir-apparent, and ruled there under his father for several years.

One of the last acts of En Jayme was to attend a Papal Council at Lyons, where he was magnificently fêted. This led to his contemplating the command of a crusade, and his fourth and last visit to Majorca was undertaken to raise recruits; but it came to nothing. The great King died at Valencia on July 27, 1276, in his seventieth year, after a reign of sixty-four years. He was buried with great pomp, but amidst the heartfelt sorrow of his people, in the monastery of Poblet, near Tarragona. Here his body rested in peace for 560 years. But in 1835 a vile mob sacked and destroyed the monastery. The King's coffin was eventually taken to the cathedral of Tarragona. It has found a final resting-place at Valencia, where his sword is also preserved.

King Jayme I. of Aragon, 'El Conquistador,' was a remarkable man—one of the greatest men of the thirteenth century. In his long reign he consolidated his dominions, while preserving the autonomy of each part which possessed a separate history and separate interests. He rendered the national assemblies more popular. He granted privileges most liberally to his subjects, encouraging agriculture and commerce. He gave an impulse to municipal government by the appointment of *jurados* and by instituting the 'Council of One Hundred' at Barcelona, a model for a popular magistracy. By the publication of his 'Libro del Consulado de Mar,' the first code of maritime law of its kind, he formed a pattern which was adopted by all other naval Powers. He compiled the *Fueros* of Aragon and Valencia, and granted those of Huesca on the model of the famous *Fueros* of Sobrarbe. He was a patron of learning; and the arts, especially architecture, flourished under his fostering care. He founded the university of Lerida. In his warlike undertakings he planned all his operations with such care and forethought that he was always successful. The institutions perfected by King Jayme were so thoroughly based on the interests and genius of the people, that they lasted, with modifications, for more than four centuries. Just, affable, and sympathetic, the memory of Jayme the Conqueror is enshrined in the hearts of the descendants of his people, and when the seventh centenary of his birth came round, on February 8, 1908, it was seen that the great King is not forgotten. In Majorca, on the day of St. Silvester, the day on which Palma was taken, there was an annual procession in which the bishop and the authorities joined, with En Jayme's banner borne before them; followed by a high Mass in the cathedral, when all the people prayed for the soul of their beloved King. Relics of King Jayme, consisting of his saddle, a stirrup, and a helmet, were long preserved at Palma. They are now in the royal armoury at Madrid; and the procession which revived old memories and aroused patriotic feelings has itself become a thing of the past.

CHAPTER V
TELLS HOW THE KING OF ARAGON TOOK UP CONRADIN'S GLOVE; HOW THE POPE'S CURSES WENT HOME TO ROOST; AND HOW EN PEDRO KEPT HIS TRYST

For fifty years after the death of Jayme I. we have the guidance of that delightful old chronicler En Ramon Muntaner, who had seen many years of active service in the field before he took up his pen to record the events of which he had personal knowledge. He was born in his father's house at Peralada, near the frontier of Catalonia and Roussillon, and thought he could just remember the great King Jayme having been his father's guest for one night. But he left his home when only eleven years of age, having been born in 1275, the year before the death of the 'Conquistador.' After knocking about the world for half a century and doing much faithful and honourable service by sea and land, the old warrior retired to a farm in the 'garden' of Valencia, called Xiluella. There, in the year 1335, and at the age of sixty, he tells us that a vision appeared to him when he was sleeping on his couch. It was revealed to him that it was God's will that he should arise and write the story of his life and of the great marvels he had witnessed, that they might be made manifest. So the veteran wrote his story for the honour of God, of His blessed Mother, and of the House of Aragon. Muntaner is the Froissart of Catalonia.[5]

Transparently honest and trustworthy, the warrior-historian is a sure guide through the very complicated events in which Jayme II., the first separate King of Majorca, and his sons were more or less concerned during those fifty years of which Muntaner treats.

Pedro III. succeeded to the kingdoms of Aragon and Valencia and the county of Barcelona. His brother Jayme was present at the coronation at Zaragoza. Jayme then proceeded to Majorca, and was crowned King in the cathedral. He had practically ruled the Balearic islands for several years before his father's death, and was very popular with the islanders. He also took possession of his Continental dominions of Roussillon, Cerdaña, Conflent, and Montpellier.

The two brothers appear to have had very different dispositions. Pedro was ambitious, bold almost to rashness, and enterprising. Jayme was more inclined to a life of quiet and peace. Both had been devotedly loyal to their great father during his life. Circumstances almost forced upon Pedro a very glorious career of successful warfare in a good cause. The same circumstances placed Jayme in a position of extreme difficulty as regarded his relations with his brother.

Jayme I. was scarcely in his grave when the troubles commenced in the south of Italy and Sicily with which the House of Aragon became so closely connected. They arose entirely from the malignant hatred of the Popes for that great and enlightened Emperor, Frederick II., King of Sicily, and from their unscrupulous ambition. When the Emperor was succeeded by his son Manfred, the papal enmity was transferred to him; and the Pope appealed to all the Christian kings to drive him from his dominions. St. Louis of France refused to perpetrate this iniquity, being a friend of the late Emperor. King Edward of England refused, his aunt having married Frederick II. The King of Castille refused. Above all, the King of Aragon denounced the scheme, his wife Constance being a daughter of Manfred.

Still the Pope succeeded in his wicked design in an unexpected way. The Kings of England, France, and of the Romans, and Charles of Anjou, brother of the King of France, had married four sisters, the daughters of the Count of Provence.[6] All were queens except the wife of Charles of Anjou, and she was the eldest. This filled her with envy and jealousy, and she tormented her husband until he bethought him of a way to make her a queen by doing the Pope's dirty work and becoming the papal King of Sicily. So, without his brother's knowledge or consent, he went to Rome, and made the offer on condition that the treasure of the Church was placed at his disposal. The compact was made, the Pope crowned Charles, and he raised an army to invade the territory of King Manfred.

Muntaner says truly that Manfred was one of the most valiant kings in the world. He assembled his army and met the invading host under Charles of Anjou near the frontier of his dominions. The battle raged fiercely, and Manfred would have been victorious had not bribes, applied with the help of the treasure of the Church, turned the scale. There was treachery. The gallant King was slain, his army was scattered, and the Pope's *protégé* was enabled to occupy Naples and overrun Sicily, which was occupied by the licentious soldiery of Charles of Anjou. The papal nominee used his success with unrelenting cruelty. The wife and children of Manfred were shut up in a dungeon. Conradin, the nephew and heir, came from Germany with a small force, but was defeated and taken prisoner. Charles caused him to be beheaded at Naples, and, as is well known, the young prince, when on the scaffold, threw his glove into the crowd, praying that some one would take it to King Pedro of Aragon, who would avenge his wrongs.

Pedro III. took up Conradin's glove to some purpose. His death was the last success of Charles of Anjou. The Pope had cursed the family of the good Emperor. Never did curses more persistently come home to roost.

The Catalans were fast becoming an important naval power in the Mediterranean, and their King fostered its growth with care. He established arsenals and dockyards at Barcelona, Tortosa, Cullera, and Valencia, and ordered smaller yards to be formed at every port where there was anchorage for his galleys. Cullera and Tortosa were his principal dockyards. The men were so well trained, the galleys and arms were kept in such a state of efficiency, that Pedro was well able to take up Conradin's glove and to avenge the death of Manfred, the father of his beloved wife Constance.

The call soon came. The King of Aragon was moved to anger when he heard of the death of his father-in-law and of young Conradin. Before taking any steps against the usurper, he thought it well to secure himself from attacks on the side of France. His brother of Majorca was also anxious for his Continental dominions. St. Louis of France had been succeeded in 1270 by his son Philip *le Hardi*, who had married Pedro's sister. An interview was arranged between the Kings of France, Aragon, and Majorca at Toulouse. The negotiation which followed was so far satisfactory that Philip solemnly swore never to interfere in the affairs of Montpellier, and professed warm friendship for both the Aragonese Kings.

At this juncture the tyranny of the French led to the 'Sicilian Vespers.' The people rose throughout Sicily while Charles of Anjou prepared to wreak vengeance upon them, collecting a large army and fleet. The Sicilians turned to the King of Aragon, whose wife was the heir to their King, for help in their sore need, and their appeal was not in vain. He was engaged in some successful operations on the coast of Barbary, with a large, well-appointed fleet, when the message reached him. Pedro did not hesitate. He would take up Conradin's glove and defend the right. With a fair wind, he caused his fleet to shape a course for Sicily.

The King of Aragon landed at Trapani on August 28, 1282. The whole population of Sicily was overjoyed. The march from Trapani to Palermo was a triumphal procession. Pedro was crowned King of Sicily at Palermo, and immediately afterwards he marched to Messina, to resist any attempt to invade the island on the part of the French forces of Charles of Anjou.

Charles arrived before Messina with his army, where he received envoys from the King of Aragon. They told him, in the name of their master, that he was a usurper; that he knew well that he had no right to the kingdom, which belonged to the Queen of Aragon and her sons as heirs of King Manfred, and demanded that he should leave it. Charles replied defiantly, and Pedro, calling all the able-bodied men of Sicily to arms, prepared to advance to Messina and attack the usurper, who was besieging the town, by sea and land.

It is here necessary to give some account of a peculiar body of light infantry which formed an important part of the Aragonese army, and was now destined to take a very active lead in sending the Pope's curses home to roost.

The origin of these troops, called *Almogavares*, is said by Desclot and others to be as follows: After Spain was overrun by the Arabs, many of the fugitive inhabitants took refuge in fastnesses of the mountains, whence they made incursions into the open country, their necessities obliging them to make no distinction between friends and enemies. In course of time these outlaws were organised into tribes, and generations of men who were always leading lives of danger and hardship produced a race of most formidable fighting soldiers. The Kings of Aragon transformed these fierce wanderers into a new military organisation. They became fanatically loyal troops, while retaining their old customs and habits. They were divided into companies, each under a captain, named *almogadan*. They also had officers named *adalid*,[7] who were guides for the routes, and who also had authority to judge of what occurred in the forays, and to divide the spoils. The dress of an *almogarave* consisted of a smock, breeches, leather gaiters, hide sandals called *abarcas*, a sort of knapsack on the back to hold a day's food, and a belt round the waist with a dagger, and a small bag containing flint and steel. The *almogarave* never shaved and never cut his hair, which was confined in a net. His arms were a short lance and a few darts slung on his back. In an ambush or night attack they first made innumerable sparks with their flints and steels in all directions, then rushed furiously upon their enemy with the war-cry of '*Desparte ferres!*'[8] and shouts of '*Al mugabar.*' This word may be allied to the Hebrew '*muhavar*,' which means a companion.

The *almogavares* were an exceedingly formidable body of light infantry. Pedro sent 2,000 to Messina by forced marches, while he followed with the main strength of his army. Arriving at Messina, they were received into the town, but the inhabitants were in despair at their ragged and wild appearance, and feared that men like these could never cope with the soldiers of Charles. Their answer was, 'We will show you what we are like'; and at dawn they sallied out of Messina and attacked the besieging army with such fury that it was thrown into confusion. Charles of Anjou thought the whole Aragonese army was upon him. He hastily ordered his troops to embark, and fled to the opposite coast; but his rearguard was cut to pieces and all his baggage was captured. The galleys of Aragon then attacked the usurper's fleet off Nicotera, capturing many vessels and driving the rest on shore. A body of *almogavares* was next taken over to the coast of Apulia, where they defeated a French force at Catona, the Comte d'Alençon, brother of the King of France, being among the slain. Thus was Sicily permanently delivered from the yoke of Charles of Anjou, and restored to its rightful heir, the daughter of Manfred. King Pedro himself crossed the Strait of Messina and captured several towns in Apulia, including Reggio.

Charles of Anjou, beaten in every encounter, sent a challenge to the King of Aragon, proposing that their quarrel should be settled by one combat, a hundred on each side. Pedro consented, and it was arranged that the battle should take place at Bordeaux, King Edward I. of England being the umpire.

Before returning to Aragon to prepare for this duel, En Pedro made a very important appointment. En Roger de Lauria had been brought up with the King as a boy, and his mother was for many years in attendance on Queen Constance. En Roger had since proved himself to be a valiant and enterprising commander and an expert sailor. The King appointed him Admiral of Catalonia, Valencia, and Sicily; and he was by far the greatest admiral of the thirteenth century. When it was known that En Roger had received his *bâton* there was great rejoicing in the fleet and in the city of Messina, a week of holidays, dancing, and festivity, ending with a General Council, when the King delivered a farewell speech. Next to En Roger de Lauria, the most trusted naval captains were En Ramon Marquet and En Berenguer Mallol. Leaving the kingdom of Sicily in peace and well ordered, King Pedro sailed from Trapani with his two captains and only four galleys, arriving safely at Barcelona. The rest of the great fleet remained under the command of En Roger.

The beaten usurper went crying to Pope Martin for more curses against the rightful heirs of Sicily, and for more treasure from the coffers of Holy Church. The requests of Charles of Anjou were promptly complied with. The King of Aragon was excommunicated, a crusade was declared against him, and more funds were supplied to the papal King, who then left Rome and proceeded to his nephew of France. Pedro III., with all his bishops and a loyal and united people at his back, cared nothing for the Pope's curses. The Pope further gave orders to his Legate to absolve King Philip of France from all the promises he had ever made to the Aragonese kings; and to call upon him to engage in an iniquitous crusade against his neighbour and brother-in-law.

The first act of hostility was the equipment of a fleet at Marseilles with the object of seeking out and destroying the galleys commanded by En Roger de Lauria. The Provençal Admiral Cornut had with him twenty-two well-armed galleys, and shaped a course to Malta, where he encountered the fleet of Lauria, numbering only eighteen sail. The two fleets, in order of battle, rammed each other, and then came to close quarters. The Catalans were well trained in the use of the crossbow. Every shot told, and before long the decks of the Provençal ships were cleared. The admiral of the Marseilles fleet, with his friends and officers, perished in the thick of the fight. All the twenty-two galleys became prizes to Lauria, and the glorious news was at once sent to Syracuse, spreading joy and gladness throughout the island. The castle and town of Malta surrendered, and both Malta and Gozo were transferred from the possession of Charles of Anjou to that of the Aragonese rulers of Sicily. The return of the fleet to Sicily was the occasion of great rejoicing. En Roger was received as a hero at Syracuse,

Aci Reale, Taormina, and most of all at Messina, where the victorious fleet finally anchored. Such was the next reply to the Pope's curses.

Very earnest requests had been made by both parties to King Edward of England to act as umpire for the proposed duel, for he was known to be the most upright and just prince in Christendom. Both Pedro and Charles had sworn to be on the spot on the day appointed. But it came to the knowledge of King Edward that his cousin of France and his papal uncle were not playing the game. Instead of a hundred knights, they were coming to the neighbourhood of Bordeaux with an army of twelve thousand men, intending to kill En Pedro and all who came with him. Edward therefore resolved not to come, for he would be unable to ensure fair play; and he sent to tell the King of Aragon that, under the circumstances, he was absolved from his oath. En Pedro then set out upon the wildest and most romantic adventure that ever was undertaken even in that age of romance. The French King and his uncle of Anjou had actually come to Bordeaux with a large army; had set out the field of combat, with a stand at one end for the King of England as umpire, and a chapel at the other. The English Seneschal of Bordeaux received them with courtesy, but told them the reason why his master would not be present. In spite of the warnings from King Edward and of his own intelligence, En Pedro was determined that nothing should prevent him from keeping his oath to be at the appointed place on the appointed day. He knew that his own people would never consent to his entering upon such a madcap adventure. Whatever was done must be done in profound secrecy. Pedro had an envoy in Bordeaux, named Gilbert de Cruilles, who was empowered to treat with the English Seneschal; but even he was not in the secret at first, though he constantly sent reports of the French proceedings.

The King of Aragon went to Jaca, in the heart of the Pyrenees, with a few attendants, and sent for a horse-dealer of his acquaintance, upon whose secrecy and probity he could rely. This merchant, named Domingo de la Figuera, was a man of considerable influence, carrying on an extensive trade in horses between Bordeaux and Navarre, Castille, and Aragon. He knew intimately every road and path in the Pyrenees, every man who frequented them, and every post and tavern. The King explained his wild scheme to En Domingo. The horse-dealer was to provide twenty-seven horses, nine to be stationed along the road from Jaca to Bordeaux, nine on the route from Bordeaux to Navarre, and nine for a return journey in Castille. En Domingo was to ride post as master, while the King and a young knight named Bernardo de Peratallada, son of the envoy Gilbert de Cruilles, were to follow as his servants, suitably dressed, with light saddle-bags. They were to ride at a great pace all day, stopping at an inn at dusk. At early dawn they were to mount fresh horses, which were to be ready saddled. The King was to act as a squire, holding the stirrup of En

Domingo when he mounted, serving him at table, while En Bernardo fed the horses; and then the King and En Bernardo were to sup together at a table apart, before lying down to sleep. En Domingo was to post the horses at proper distances in charge of men on whom he could rely, but who were not to be in the secret. En Domingo undertook to arrange all these details, and a day was fixed for departure which would bring them to Bordeaux on the eve of the appointed time. Not a soul was in the secret save the King himself, En Domingo, and En Bernardo.

All being settled, the King went to Zaragoza to pass a few days with his wife and children, taking a tender farewell of them on his departure; but they little knew why he took leave of them with more affection than usual and to what risks he was about to expose himself.

All being prepared, the three companions started from Jaca. The King wore strong gaiters, a doublet of canvas, and over all a very old and shabby smock, with a cap, and a kind of hood concealing his face. En Bernardo was dressed in the same way; while En Domingo rode as their master in a handsome dress and broad hat, fine gauntlets, and with a smart saddle-cloth. En Bernardo carried a great sack, containing six loaves of bread to be eaten during the day, without stopping. At the first inn the people asked En Domingo why he came so late, to which he replied that it was to keep the horses out of the sun; and while he conversed with people outside, the King got the supper ready and En Bernardo fed the horses. The King then held the ewer of water for En Domingo's hands, served him at table, and when En Bernardo came in, he and the King had their suppers together at another table, then lying down and sleeping until dawn. Fresh horses were ready, and they went off at a gallop. On the third evening they were within a league of Bordeaux, where they stopped at a house whose owner was a friend of En Domingo. Here they had supper and rested for the night. At dawn they were mounted again and riding to the field, it being the actual day appointed for the duel. The master of the house went to Gilbert de Cruilles, who was lodged near, to tell him what had happened, and both rode off to the field, where, to his amazement, Gilbert saw the King and his own son. En Pedro took him aside and told him to go at once to the English Seneschal of Bordeaux and tell him that a knight from the King of Aragon had arrived and wished for speech with him; and to ask him to bring with him his notary, six knights whom he could trust, and no one else.

En Gilbert went at once to the Seneschal, who was with the King of France, and delivered his message. The Seneschal then told the King that a knight of Aragon had come who desired to speak with him. 'Go,' said the King, 'and afterwards come and tell me what he had to say.' So the Seneschal went at once, with the best notary at the English Court and with six knights of distinction. He found the King on the field, who saluted him courteously, saying: 'Sir Seneschal, I am here on the part of the King of Aragon, this being the day on which he and King Charles have sworn to encounter each other in this field. I therefore ask you whether the King can come in safety, in the event of his appearing this day?' The Seneschal replied, in the name of the King of England, that he could in no way guarantee his safety; for he knew for a certainty that, if he came, he, and all who came with him, would be killed, that being the intention of the King of France and his uncle Charles, who were here with twelve thousand armed horsemen. 'Very good,' replied En Pedro. 'Let this be written down by the notary and witnessed'; and the Seneschal gave the order for this to be done. The notary wrote it down, and when he came to the name of the Aragonese knight the Seneschal asked him for it. 'Can all here be trusted?' asked En Pedro. 'Certainly,' was the answer, 'on the faith of the King of England.' 'Then, Seneschal, you know me,' said the King of Aragon, and he threw back his hood. The Seneschal recognised him at once, and went down on his knee, saying, 'Oh, sir, what is this that you have done?' 'I have come here,' replied the King, 'to keep my oath; and I desire that all you have told me and all I do may be written down in full by the notary, certifying that I have come this day in person, and that I have searched out all the field.' He then rode down the field and to every part of it, in the presence of the witnesses, and while the notary was writing. After he had galloped up and down several times, he dismounted at the chapel and offered up thanks to God that he had been enabled to keep his oath. They then all rode back to the house of the host of the previous night, and the King dismounted and went in to thank and take leave of his hostess, who was overcome by the honour when she heard who her guest was. En Pedro sent a request through the Seneschal to the King of England that his host might receive a suitable reward. He also requested that fair copies of the notary's statement might be drawn up, one to be delivered to the Seneschal for transmission to the King of England, and the other to Gilbert de Cruilles for the King of Aragon. The perilous return journey was then commenced, the Seneschal accompanying the party for about a league. On taking his leave he told En Domingo on no account to return by the way he came, nor even by Navarre, because the King of France had sent orders in all directions to seize anyone in the service of the King of Aragon.

The travellers took the road to Castille, travelling with great speed, not a single arrangement made by En Domingo failing them in their need. They went by Soria and crossed the Aragonese frontier at Moanquels. On reaching Calatayud the King found that the news of his gallant adventure had preceded him, and the people were in transports of joy. At Zaragoza there were processions headed by the bishops and clergy, in spite of the Pope's excommunication, to offer up thanks for their chivalrous King's safety.

When the Seneschal considered that the King of Aragon was safe, he went to King Philip of France and his uncle Charles of Anjou and told them all that had taken place. On hearing such news they made the sign of the cross more than a hundred times, and were dumfounded. Then they went to the field to see the marks of King Pedro's horse's hoofs; and Philip expressed admiration at the chivalrous daring of his brother-in-law. Next day he broke up his camp and marched away to Toulouse, with his uncle of Anjou. During four days there were festivities at Zaragoza, joined in by the Queen and her children, when the two faithful companions of the King, En Bernardo and En Domingo, were fêted and richly rewarded. Then En Gilbert de Cruilles arrived from Bordeaux with the attested copy of the notary's statement, and with the news of the astonishment and departure of the French King and his uncle of Anjou: how they kept watch all night, expecting to be attacked, and how they went to look at En Pedro's horse's hoof-marks; which gave rise to much laughter at Zaragoza. In this way did the brave and chivalrous King of Aragon keep his tryst.

CHAPTER VI
TELLS HOW THE QUEEN OF ARAGON WENT TO SICILY WITH HER SONS, HOW ADMIRAL LAURIA WON NEW VICTORIES, AND HOW MORE OF THE POPE'S CURSES WENT HOME TO ROOST

The connection of Majorca and its Princes with the operations of the Aragonese in Sicily was so intimate that their story would not be clear without some account of the recovery of Manfred's kingdom for his descendants. We now come to a time when Jayme II. of Majorca was placed in a most difficult and embarrassing dilemma, owing to the position of his Continental possessions between France and Aragon.

After his return from the perilous journey to Bordeaux, Pedro III., with the concurrence of the Cortes of Aragon and Catalonia, came to a very important decision. His queen, daughter and heir of King Manfred, was to proceed to her Sicilian possessions and thus ensure the loyalty and devotion of the people who had been delivered from the tyranny of Charles of Anjou by her husband. She was to be accompanied by her two younger sons, Jayme and Federigo. The latter was quite a young boy, there being an interval of seven years between the two brothers. The eldest son, Alfonso, was to remain with his father. As a measure of State policy it was wise and judicious. But the separation was a sacrifice to duty and a cause of grief and anxiety both to En Pedro and to Queen Constance. They never saw each other again.

A fleet was fitted out at Barcelona with great care, and every known appliance for ensuring a safe voyage was brought into requisition. Even the use of compasses is mentioned by Muntaner. The discovery has usually been attributed to one Flavio Gioia of Amalfi and to the year 1302. But here we have evidence of their use a quarter of a century earlier; while at about the same time Raimundo Lulio of Majorca (I quote from a note of Antonio de Borafull) wrote these words in his work 'De Contemplatione': 'Sicut acus per naturam vertitur ad septentrionem dum sit tacta a magnete.' The ships, thus quite exceptionally provided and well manned with Catalan crossbowmen, were to be under the guidance of those trusty sea-captains, Ramon Marquet and Berenguer Mallol.

There were religious services, but En Pedro felt the parting with his beloved Constance so deeply that he could not go with her to the ship. He shut himself up alone for several hours. It was his brother Jayme, the King of Majorca, who accompanied the Queen and his two nephews to the ship and saw them safe on board. The two brothers spent that evening together, and next day the King of Majorca set out for Perpignan. Up to this time En Pedro and En Jayme were on friendly terms. After a successful voyage the Queen and her sons arrived at Palermo. They were received with extraordinary enthusiasm, and messengers with the joyful news were sent all over the island. This return to the home of her childhood, with such a reception, must have been a cause of delight for the daughter of Manfred, though not unmixed with sorrow. For one of her sisters still lingered in a dungeon at Naples, while the rest of her family had been relieved by death. A vessel was at once sent back to Barcelona with news of the safe arrival. The Queen had a wise and loyal councillor in John of Procida, and by his advice she assembled the Parliament of the kingdom at Palermo. A letter was read from Pedro III., announcing that he had sent his beloved wife to take her place as rightful Queen of Sicily. All the members swore allegiance to her and her sons amidst a scene of enthusiasm which was quite unanimous. The proceedings terminated with a blessing from the Queen and a prayer for the well-being of the representatives and of the people they represented, who returned to their homes. The Queen and her sons then proceeded by land to Messina.

In the Admiral Roger de Lauria Sicily had a defender whose invariable success since the battle of Malta had filled his enemies with dread. The young Prince En Jayme also gained a victory at sea, and reduced the two castles still held by Charles's garrisons, Augusta and Cefalu.

The admiral was ready to sail from Messina in June 1284 with forty armed galleys, besides smaller vessels. With this force he gained one of his most brilliant victories. He shaped a course for Naples, and formed in line of battle about two bow-shots from the mole, as a defiance and a challenge. Charles of Anjou was intriguing at Rome, but his eldest son and heir was in Naples, and ready to accept the challenge. His followers were not equally willing. The name of Roger de Lauria was one of dread, and the Neapolitans held back. The younger Charles was furious. He embarked himself, and shame obliged his officers to follow. A fleet of thirty-eight galleys and many smaller vessels was got ready, and came forth to encounter the terrible Roger de Lauria. A battle raged in the Bay of Naples from nine in the morning until dusk, but as usual victory attended on the banners of the admiral of Aragon. The Prince's galley was surrounded and boarded by En Roger himself, to whom Charles, after a long and brave resistance, was forced to surrender. The admiral said to the usurper's son: 'You must do two things. If not, be sure that the death of Conradin will be avenged.' The Prince answered that he would do anything to save his own life. 'The first thing,' continued the admiral, 'is that you order the daughter of King Manfred to be released from her prison and brought safely on board my galley.' This demand was complied with. The long-imprisoned princess was taken from the Castel del Novo and brought safely on board the flagship, where the admiral joyfully received the sister of his Queen, kneeling before her and treating her with all honour and respect. 'The second thing,' continued he to Charles, 'is that you deliver up to me the town and castle of Ischia.' This also was done.

The victorious fleet then returned to Messina with the released princess and the captive prince. Never had there been seen such rejoicings in Messina as greeted the admiral on his return. The Queen and her sons went on board the galley to receive their long-imprisoned relation. It was a most affecting scene. The two sisters embraced each other, weeping for joy mingled with sorrow. Since they had seen each other their father Manfred and their cousin Conradin had been killed; their mother and all the rest of their family had died in prison. The crowd of spectators was equally moved when the sisters, with the young princes, walked together from the landing-stage to the palace. Charles was sent to the castle of Matagrifone.

The Sicilian Parliament met at Messina soon afterwards and decreed the death of the younger Charles, as a reprisal for the death of Conradin. He would certainly have been executed if the young Prince En Jayme had not interfered, preferring the more generous course of returning good for evil. Charles was confined for some time in the castle of Cefalu, and eventually removed, by order of King Pedro, to a prison at Barcelona.

The Pope's curses kept coming home to roost, but this failed to divert him from his vindictive course. His *protégé*, Charles of Anjou, was at Rome when the disastrous news arrived, and must have felt that retribution was overtaking him. The usurper hurried back to Naples, but died at Foggio on January 7, 1283. The Pope was furious, and was more liberal than ever with his curses. He placed the kingdom of Aragon under an interdict, decreed the dethronement of En Pedro, declared a crusade against him, made Charles of Valois, the younger son of France, King of Aragon, ordering him to be crowned, and called upon the King of France to attack Aragon with all his forces by land and sea. He further absolved Philip of France from keeping his oaths and treaties made with his brother-in-law of Aragon. A papal Legate was to accompany the invading army.

En Pedro sent an embassy to Rome, consisting of grave and learned counsellors. In a dignified speech their spokesman remonstrated with the Pope and his cardinals. They were, however, obdurate, and all the answer they would give was that the Holy See could do no wrong. Finally the ambassadors made a solemn appeal from an unjust vicegerent to St. Peter himself and to God, who would defend the right, and so departed.

En Pedro prepared to defend his country, confident in the loyalty of his people and the justice of his cause. He had an interview with his nephew Sancho, the usurping King of Castille, who promised to give him all the assistance in his power. He also discussed the situation with his brother of

Majorca. They were several days together at Gerona. The position was a most difficult one. If Jayme opposed the advance of the French army through his Continental dominions their permanent loss to the house of Aragon would be inevitable. If he offered no opposition he would be giving an advantage to his brother's enemy. The brothers chose what appeared to be the least of two evils. En Jayme was to allow the French army to march across his territories, and to avoid any action which would furnish a pretext for their annexation.

Philip (*le Hardi*) can hardly have had any heart in the enterprise which was forced upon him by the Pope. His eldest son, who had a strong feeling of regard and admiration for his uncle En Pedro, openly disapproved. When his younger brother, Charles of Valois, talked of himself as King of Aragon, Philip said to him: 'You, little brother, are not fit to take the place of our uncle. You are scarcely fit to be king of what is under your cap. You will never be King of Aragon.' There was an angry quarrel, and their father had to separate them. But Charles got the name of King Cap, '*le roi du chapeau*.' Nevertheless, it was generally believed that little Aragon would have no chance against the whole power of France, and that the campaign could have but one result, and would be over in a few weeks. The oriflamme was unfurled, and a great army, led by the King of France and accompanied by the Cardinal Legate, advanced to the Catalonian frontier. A formidable fleet was also equipped, to overpower the naval forces of Aragon and to keep up the supplies for the army in the bay of Rosas. In April 1285 King Philip encamped with his army at Perpignan. The French were constantly harassed by night attacks from the Aragonese; and at last, after a fortnight of hesitation, Philip determined to attempt a passage into Catalonia by the hill of Panisars. Here he was attacked on all sides, suffering very serious losses. Then young Philip turned to his brother and said: 'See now, pretty brother, how glad your subjects are to see you!' His father overheard the sneer and was very angry. 'Hold your tongue, Philip. They will be made to repent what they are doing.' 'Ah, Sire,' answered his son, 'I mourn for your honour and for the evil that is being done you. The Pope and cardinals have brought this upon you, and have made my brother king of the wind, while they take their pleasure, caring little for the danger and evil with which you are menaced.' The King was silent, for he knew very well that his son had merely spoken the truth. But it was too late to repent and turn back.

Following the advice of some monks, Philip got possession of another pass, known as the 'Collado de Masona,' and his army was thus enabled to invade Catalonia. The little town of Peralada was taken after a brave resistance, and siege was laid to the city of Gerona. But the French army was harassed by incessant attacks, and was entirely dependent for supplies on the navy which guarded the transports conveying provisions from Marseilles and Cette to the bay of Rosas. Here was the weak point.

En Pedro received information from the gallant sea-captains Marquet and Malliol, who were ever on the watch, that the French King had 160 galleys; that his admiral kept sixty well-armed in the port of San Felio; that another fifty cruised between San Felio and the bay of Rosas; while twenty-five plied between those ports and Marseilles with provisions. Another twenty-five remained in the bay of Rosas, under the command of a brave knight, M. de Lodève. The proposal of the Catalan captains was to watch for an opportunity when the other cruisers were out of sight, and to fall upon the twenty-five French galleys in Rosas Bay at early dawn. The King approved of their daring scheme, and at the same time he sent to Sicily for the Admiral Roger de Lauria to come with sixty galleys and attack the rest of the French fleet.

Marquet and Malliol set out on their enterprise with eleven galleys and two small vessels. But never were crews better disciplined or more carefully trained. They made sail for the Cape of Creus, where they ascertained that the twenty-five French galleys were in Rosas Bay. As soon as the Catalans came in sight, M. de Lodève sent fifteen galleys to dispute their entrance into the bay; while he intended to manœuvre with the rest so as to cut off their retreat, that none might escape. Marquet and Malliol formed in close order to prevent the enemy from dividing their line, and ran on with a view of boarding. Their trust was in their crossbowmen. The Catalans considered that no one was a crossbowman unless he was so familiar with every part of his weapon that he could make it or repair it. Each man carried a box containing all the tools necessary; and the Catalans were so constantly trained in the use of the crossbow that no other people could compete with them.

The Catalan captains manœuvred so as to secure the greatest advantage for their special weapon. Every shot told; while the French, with swords and lances, were unable to return the attack, being shot down when they attempted to board. When the French decks were nearly cleared, Marquet and Malliol ordered the trumpets to be sounded as a signal for his galleys to separate under oars and attack the enemy on their broadsides. Then began an unequal combat, the Catalans boarding at the sword's point, while the French had already suffered so severely as only to be able to offer a feeble resistance. The whole of the twenty-five galleys were captured, with a loss of upwards of four thousand on the part of the French, and of barely a hundred on the Catalan side. This naval battle was a combination of consummate seamanship with consummate gunnery practice, the one of little avail without the other.

M. de Lodève had sent a boat to apprise fifty French galleys cruising in the offing of the approach of the Catalans, and they made sail for Rosas Bay.

The winds were light and baffling, and the Catalans, with their prizes, were only sighted after the battle was over. The French admiral could not overtake his victorious enemy, but he stationed twenty-five more galleys in Rosas Bay, and returned to San Felio.

As soon as the Admiral Roger de Lauria received his orders he left Messina with sixty-six well-armed galleys in search of the French fleet, steering for a rendezvous at the island of Cabrera. Here he received tidings from the Captains Marquet and Malliol that there were eighty-five French galleys in Rosas Bay. They informed the Admiral that they would join him, with sixteen galleys, off a cape known as Aygua Freda, near some small islets called the Formigueras.[9] Admiral Lauria ordered that each galley should have three lights ready—one in the bows, another amidships, and a third at the stern. If the French fleet approached at night, all were to be suddenly lighted, that the enemy might believe each light to be on a separate vessel. Towards dawn the French fleet approached, and all the lights suddenly appeared between the fleet and the shore. Before it was broad daylight Lauria had entirely defeated his adversary, capturing fifty-four galleys, driving fifteen on shore, and putting twenty-five Genoese auxiliaries to flight. Marquet and Malliol completed the rout by capturing the remaining French galleys in Rosas Bay, and taking or destroying all the stores and provisions for the French army. The admiral proceeded to Barcelona, having by this great naval victory obtained complete command of the sea.

There was nothing left for the great French army but an ignominious flight. The Cardinal Legate said that the Aragonese must be devils. King Philip told him that they were nothing of the kind, but brave and loyal soldiers, defending their King against an unjust invasion; and he expressed his regret that he had ever undertaken it at the Pope's urgent call. The Cardinal remained silent. En Pedro assembled his army on the hill of Panisars to intercept the retreat. The French King raised the siege of Gerona and fell back on Peralada with the remnant of his forces. Many had died of sickness, while the losses in numerous harassing encounters had been most serious. The King of France was very ill, anxiety and regret hastening his end. Feeling that he was dying, he sent for his son, and said: 'You were wiser than I. Had I followed your advice I should not now be on my deathbed; nor would the many brave men have been lost who have died and will die in this war. Send a message to your uncle of Aragon and ask him to allow my body to pass with yourself and your brother. For I am certain that it rests with him whether a single Frenchman shall ever return, dead or alive.' The dying King then obtained a promise from his son that he would be a friend and protector of his brother Charles. The King died on September 30, 1285, in the house of a knight named Vilanova, about two miles from Peralada. When En Pedro received the message from the young King Philip he sent orders that the late King's body was to be allowed to pass with its escort, and requested his brother of Majorca to meet it with a body of cavalry and protect it from attacks. For Lauria and his sailors were watching on one side, and bands of wild *almogavares* on the other. But safety could only be assured to those who passed with the corpse and the oriflamme. The Count of Foix with five hundred horsemen went first, then the young King and his brother with the oriflamme, following their father's body. The Cardinal Legate came close behind, careful of his own safety. He said that the rest would go to Paradise. The Aragonese could no longer be restrained, and fell furiously on the remainder of the retreating host and on the baggage. The Cardinal was so terrified that he died of fright a few days afterwards; while the King of Majorca escorted his nephew, the young King of France, with his brother Charles and the body of the late King, through his dominions.

The victorious King En Pedro, after making liberal grants to the towns of Peralada and Gerona, returned to Barcelona with his principal nobles. On the same day the Admiral Roger de Lauria arrived with the fleet, and there was great rejoicing.

This time the Pope's curses went home to roost with a vengeance. En Pedro was firmer on his throne than ever. Sicily was safe. The Pope's *protégé* was in prison at Barcelona. The Pope's King of Aragon was only king of what was under his own cap. The Pope's machinations were scattered to the winds.

Yet the papal intrigues continued to cause trouble and dissensions.

Jayme II., the King of Majorca, was obliged, owing to the exigencies of the times, to reside in his Continental dominions. By his wife, Esclaramunda, sister of the Count of Foix, he had four sons, Jayme, Sancho, Fernando, and Felipe, and two daughters named Isabel and Sancha. Isabel was the wife of the Infante Juan Manuel, brother of the King of Castille. Sancha married King Robert of Naples. Jayme and Sancho were at Paris, detained by the King of France, practically as hostages. Fernando's age was then about eight, the elder brothers ten and twelve.

There had been an understanding between the brothers Pedro and Jayme during the war, and communications had passed between them respecting the safe passage of the French King's body, and on other matters. Soon after the final rout of the French strange tidings reached En Pedro from his agents in Italy. He was assured that the Pope would induce the King of France to seize Majorca, and that Jayme would be forced to give his consent, because his two sons were in the French King's power in Paris, and Montpellier, Roussillon, and Conflent would otherwise be taken from him. En Pedro resolved to prevent this. He did not see how, in the face of these threats, his brother could refuse, and he must therefore act promptly; but he sent a letter to his brother Jayme explaining the motives of his action. The force destined for Majorca was placed under the command of the King's eldest son, Alfonso, and consisted of knights, men-at-arms, and two thousand *almogavares*.

The King of Aragon was incensed with his nephew Sancho IV., the usurping King of Castille, because he had broken his promise and given him no help whatever in the war with France. Fernando, the eldest son of Alfonso X., had died before his father, leaving two sons, Alfonso and Fernando, known as the 'Infantes of La Cerda.' The next son, Sancho, had usurped the throne, and the 'Infantes de La Cerda' had escaped into Aragon. En Pedro was having them educated in the castle of Jativa in Valencia. He was so angry with Sancho that he contemplated setting up the eldest Infante as a claimant for the throne of Castille. Having taken leave of his son on the eve of his departure for Majorca, En Pedro commenced a journey to Jativa to see the Infantes of La Cerda. He was feeling unwell when he started, and on reaching the town of Villafranca de Panales he was in a high fever. His son was on board, but had not sailed, when he got the news. He hurried to Villafranca, but his father ordered him to return to his ship and make sail at once. Receiving his father's blessing, the young Prince departed and embarked at the port of Salou. He landed with his forces at Porrasa, and no resistance was made to his occupation of the capital of Majorca. En Pedro was dying. He had made his will and received the Sacraments, but neither wife nor sons were at his bedside. He died on November 11, 1285, and was buried in the abbey of Santa Creus, about twenty miles from Villafranca. His great admiral, Roger de Lauria, died a few years afterwards, and his body was laid to rest near that of the King he had served so well. In 1835 a vile mob of ruffians destroyed the church and scattered the remains to the winds. By his wife Constance he left four sons and two daughters. The eldest succeeded him as Alfonso III. The second succeeded his brother as Jayme II. Federigo, the third, was King of Sicily. The fourth was Pedro. Of the daughters, Isabel was Queen of Portugal, and Violante of Naples.

Pedro III., if not equal in all respects to his father, was a great king. Fortune smiled upon him. He was happy in all relations of life. His career was one long romance. Chivalrous to recklessness, he was at the same time prudent and circumspect—a rare combination. Even in his wild gallop into imminent peril at Bordeaux he thought out every part of the enterprise down to the minutest detail. He was invariably well served, and invariably successful. This cannot be ascribed to luck. A king who succeeds in all he undertakes must have rare gifts of head and heart to plan out the details of his undertakings and to secure the sympathy and devotion of those who serve him. Pedro was thus gifted, while his administrative ability ensured the prosperity of his country. Under him Aragon became a great naval Power, and Sicily was freed from a foreign yoke.

CHAPTER VII
TELLS HOW YOUNG FEDERIGO HELD SICILY AGAINST ALL ODDS, HOW THE CATALAN COMPANY WENT TO THE EAST, AND HOW JAYME OF MAJORCA WAS RESTORED TO HIS ISLAND HOME

The news of the King's death was at once sent to Majorca and to Sicily. Alfonso was only in his twenty-second year—an impulsive, quick-tempered youth, intolerant of opposition, but not guilty of the cruelties imputed to him by some writers. He refused to surrender the Balearic Islands to his uncle again, and there was trouble about it during the five years that his reign lasted. He returned at once to Barcelona and went to mourn at his father's grave in the church of Santa Creus, previous to the coronation at Zaragoza. His brother Jayme was crowned King of Sicily at Palermo, and in a successful campaign subdued all the mainland of Calabria.

Through the intervention of King Edward I. of England, negotiations were set on foot to reconcile the King of Aragon with France and the Pope; to make a compromise with his uncle, of Majorca, and for a marriage between Alfonso III. of Aragon and the Princess Eleanor of England, a daughter of Edward I. by his second marriage. Young Alfonso spent some time with Edward I. and the intended bride at Bordeaux. He was induced to liberate Charles II. of Naples on receiving his three sons and twenty nobles of Provence in exchange. The other important questions were in a fair way of solution through the tact and diplomatic skill of the wise King Edward, when a sudden stop was put to the negotiations by the wholly unexpected death of Alfonso. A neglected tumour on his thigh brought on a fever of which he died at Barcelona when only in his twenty-seventh year. The Count of Ampudia and other great nobles at once proceeded to Sicily to announce his accession to Jayme. The new king embarked at Trapani, landed at Barcelona, and was crowned at Zaragoza as Jayme II. of Aragon. Sicily remained under the rule of Queen Constance and her son Federigo, who had now attained to years of discretion and gave promise of becoming a very able and resolute leader of men.

History is rarely quite symmetrical. One would have wished to see the noble policy of En Pedro continued as firmly and resolutely by his son. But this was not to be. Jayme II. of Aragon was weak, and fell under papal influences. There was a new Pope, and Boniface VIII. was more diplomatic. Jayme first abandoned his cousins of La Cerda, and made an alliance with the usurping Sancho of Castille. He next made his peace with

France and the Holy See, and acknowledged Charles II. of Naples as King of the Sicilies. The treaty was signed at Anagni, under the supervision of Pope Boniface. Jayme was to marry Blanche of Anjou, to give up all prisoners, and, worst shame of all, Sicily was to be handed over to the Pope again. In return the excommunication was taken off, and, in defiance of all right, Corsica and Sardinia were to be handed over to Jayme if he could drive out the Genoese and Pisans who possessed those islands; but he was to hold them in fief of the Pope.

Sicily was abandoned without the assent of En Federigo, who was now grown up and was a prince to be reckoned with. He sent Sicilian envoys to remonstrate with his brother, but without avail. He then resolved to resist the iniquity and to defy his brother and the Pope. He had against him the King of Aragon and his forces, France and Naples, and the whole influence of the papacy. He had no ally. Yet he defied them all, and swore that Sicily should be free. Many of the Catalonian nobles who revered the memory of his father rallied round the gallant young prince. He was a true son of En Pedro. Volunteers flocked to his standard. Above all, the *almogavares* were staunch to a man. En Federigo was proclaimed King of Sicily.

The Pope gave Jayme II. the titles of Gonfalonier, Admiral, and Captain-general of the Church; and, in addition to his marriage with Blanche of Anjou, he married his sister, the granddaughter of King Manfred, to the French heir of Naples.

Jayme II. received the standard of the Church at Rome, collected eighty-three galleys, and sailed to form a junction with the forces of Naples and overwhelm his brother. En Federigo had an able admiral in Conrad Doria, while Blasco de Alagon commanded the land forces. The allies made their first attack on Syracuse, where they suffered disastrous defeats both by sea and land. Charles of Naples then sent a force of 1,200 men, in fifty galleys, under the command of his son, the Prince of Tarentum, to effect a landing at Trapani. En Federigo, with some of his Catalan supporters, Moncadas and Entenzas, was ready to defend the coast. The gallant young King of Sicily led on the *almogavares*, who shouted 'Dispierto hierro!' and fell with such fury on the invaders that they broke and fled. En Federigo himself fought his way straight for his enemy's standard, and encountered the Prince of Tarentum. After a short combat the Prince was unhorsed, and would have been killed if Federigo had not protected him. He was taken prisoner and sent to the castle of Cefalu.

Charles and the Pope appealed to France for help, dispatching ambassadors with an urgent request that the King would send his brother Charles of Valois, 'the Cap King,' with a large force to invade Sicily. Accordingly he came to Naples with four thousand men, landed at Termini in Sicily, and besieged Sciacca. His people were decimated by disease, the siege had to be raised, and the expedition was a complete failure.

En Federigo had the rare gift, of surrounding himself with the ablest and most efficient men. Among these was the famous Roger de Flor. The good Emperor Frederick II. had a German falconer named Richard de Flor, who married the daughter of a rich proprietor at Brindisi. When Prince Conradin came to regain his right, Richard fought for him and was killed in the battle. All his property was confiscated and his widow was left penniless, with two boys to support, Jacobo and Roger. A ship belonging to the Knights Templars, and commanded by a Serjeant Friar named Vassayll, was wintering at Brindisi when Roger was about eight years old. The little fellow went up and down the rigging with such agility that Vassayll took a fancy for him, and persuaded his mother to let him go to sea and learn a sailor's duties. By the time he was twenty he had become a very expert seaman, and the Master of the Temple conferred on him the mantle of the Order. He was then given the command of a large ship called the *Falcon*. Friar Roger de Flor soon acquired renown as a very able naval commander. He was captain of another ship, called the *Oliveta*, when he entered the harbour of Messina and offered his services to En Federigo. He was most cordially received, and he swore allegiance to the young King of Sicily, with all his crew. His first service was to capture several large Neapolitan vessels laden with wheat and other supplies, with which the garrisons of Syracuse, Augusta, and Lentini were to be provisioned. He also captured much treasure, enabling him to make liberal presents to the nobles and to pay the wages of the garrisons. For these services the King made him Vice-Admiral of Sicily.

The Neapolitans were besieging Messina by land and sea, led by Robert, the heir of Charles II. When the town was almost at the point of starvation, Friar Roger de Flor, the Vice-Admiral, manned ten galleys, loaded them with corn, and waited at Syracuse for a fair wind. It came on to blow very fresh from the south, and he made sail in the night, reaching the *faro* of Messina just before dawn. By that time it was blowing very hard and a heavy sea was raging in the strait, with many cross-currents. The besieging ships saw the galleys, but feared to raise their anchors in such a sea. Friar Roger, with sails split and top masts sprung, led all the ten galleys safely into the harbour. Next day Duke Robert raised the siege.

Jayme II. of Aragon was half-hearted in this papal war against his young brother. He obtained a grant from the Cortes of Catalonia, and sailed for Sicily with fifty-six galleys. Federigo put to sea with only forty vessels, and there was a long-contested fight off Cape Orlando, a most fratricidal and unnatural strife. Jayme had with him Almenany, Cabrera, and other great Aragonese names. Round Federigo were Blasco de Alagon, Hugo Count of Ampurias, Gombau de Entenza, and others. It was a drawn battle, and, in spite of the prayers of Charles of Naples and of Pope Boniface, Jayme returned to Barcelona to fight no more. He must have been ashamed of the part he had been taking.

Very tardily the Pope came to see that all his curses in a bad cause were of no avail, and that they persistently came home to roost. He at length consented that his *protégé* of Naples should negotiate with En Federigo, and acknowledge him as King of Sicily. Charles of Naples met the King of Sicily at Calatabellota, and agreed to acknowledge him as king, and to give him his daughter Leonor for his wife. In return Federigo consented to evacuate Calabria. The marriage took place at Messina in May 1302.

A very large army remained in Sicily without employment. Friar Roger de Flor conceived the idea of offering his services to the Emperor of the East and of enlisting the Aragonese and Catalonian soldiers to fight against the Turks. Berenger de Entenza, Berenguer Rocafort, and many other Aragonese nobles and knights agreed to accompany the renowned Templar, and more than four thousand *almogavares* enlisted. An envoy was sent to Constantinople, and the Emperor Andronicus, with his son Michael, agreed to the terms proposed, including the scale of pay. Friar Roger was to be a Grand Duke and to marry the Emperor's niece; while liberal allowances were promised to his companions. Among them was our good and faithful chronicler Ramon Muntaner himself. En Federigo furnished ten galleys to transport the company of adventurers, provisioning them well, and supplying his faithful Admiral Friar Roger de Flor with necessary funds. The whole party which finally sailed for the East consisted of 1,500 cavalry, 4,000 *almogavares*, 1,000 other foot-soldiers, besides wives and children. There were twenty-six sail of vessels, and all embarked well pleased with the liberality of the good King of Sicily and with the prospect before them. At first the Emperor received them with much cordiality, and the company landed near Cyzicus on the Asiatic side, gaining some victories over the Turks. Friar Roger was rewarded with the title of Cæsar, which had not been conferred during four hundred years, and the company went into winter quarters at Gallipoli. Michael, the Emperor's son, had conceived an intense feeling of jealousy on account of the great honours conferred on Friar Roger. He sent an invitation to him to come to Adrianople, where he and all his companions were massacred. Another massacre was perpetrated at Constantinople; but the treacherous Greeks were defeated with great slaughter when they attacked the company at Gallipoli. The company made several retaliatory incursions, Muntaner being left in charge at Gallipoli; but there were disputes between the leaders, Entenza and Rocafort, and much need of proper guidance and of a leader acknowledged by all. At this time a Prince of Majorca began to take a part in the affairs of the company and of Greece; but before narrating his adventures we must return to the island itself and to its restoration to its rightful King.

King Jayme of Majorca had been unjustly deprived of his islands by his nephew Alfonso III., and, while constantly protesting, he was obliged to remain at Montpellier and Perpignan. But after he had made his peace with the Pope, Jayme of Aragon sought an interview with his uncle of Majorca, greeted him affectionately, and restored to him the Balearic Islands. Both the King of Majorca and the King of Aragon, uncle and nephew, were Jayme II., which might cause some confusion. For the next twelve years Jayme, the uncle, reigned peacefully in Majorca.

CHAPTER VIII
TELLS HOW KING JAYME II. AT LAST REIGNED IN PEACE, AND HOW HIS PAGE RAIMONDO LULIO ATTAINED THE CROWN OF MARTYRDOM

King Jayme II. of Majorca returned to his island dominions in 1294 with fifteen years of life before him, which he devoted to the restoration of prosperity to Majorca. He was now advanced in years, and was far better fitted for peaceful administration and the work of promoting the good of his people than for steering safely through the entanglements and difficulties caused by the war between his brother and his brother-in-law of France.

His wife, Esclaramunda of Foix, was still by his side, and his children were taking their places in the world. His eldest son, Jayme, had adopted a religious life and had become a Franciscan friar. His second son, Sancho, was therefore to be his successor, and was recognised as the heir by the Cortes of Gerona in 1302. The third son, Fernando, was one of the ablest and most valorous soldiers of that chivalrous age, with honour bright as his sword. The youngest son, Felipe, entered holy orders. The two daughters married well—Isabel to the Infante Juan Manuel of Castille, and Sancha to Robert, King of Naples.

Majorca had suffered during the usurpation of young Alfonso. Her commercial interests had been neglected, and the foreign rule had been tyrannical. At the same time the population was increasing, and there was need for the foundation of towns as centres of trade and protection in the different districts. The companions of Jayme I., forming the nobility of the island, held large estates. The twenty most prominent names were:

Surnames	Later titles
[10] Berga	——
[10] Burgues	——
[10] Canet	Viscount of Canet, 1322
Caro	Marquis of Romana, 1739
Cotoner	Marquis of Ariañy, cr. 1717
[10] Dameto	Marquis of Bellpuig, 1625
Despuig	Count of Montenegro, 1658

Fortuñy	——
[10] Morey	——
Oleza	——
[11] Puigdorfila	——
[11] Rocaberti	Count of Campofranco, 1718
Sureda	Count of Desbrull, 1717
[11] Santa Cilia	——
[11] Sant Marti	——
Togores	Count of Ayamans, 1634
Torrella	——
Truyolls	Marquis of La Torre, 1728
Villalonga	——
Zaforteza	——
[11] Gual	——

With the aid and consent of these nobles and of the Jurados, Jayme II. founded several towns which have continued to flourish to this day. One of the first was Felanitx, on the plain to the east of the capital. The next was Santañi, on the estate of Sant Marti; and the King, owing to the want of water, caused large cisterns to be constructed. Binisalem, near Inca, was founded, and is now a centre of apricot cultivation. Porreras, Sineu, and Manacor were also founded; the latter is now a flourishing town and a centre of the vine industry. Lluchmayor, the scene of his grandson's fatal overthrow, was also founded by this King. These towns formed markets and homes for the farmers of the surrounding districts.

King Jayme next established a coinage, which for its purity and accuracy of weight was very highly esteemed in all the Mediterranean commercial marts. Gold coins began to be issued in 1310, but none are now known to exist. The silver reals and double reals are handsome coins. They are excessively rare. The silver coinage began to be issued in 1300. The Mint-master was Bernardo de Oleza, whose arms were gules a rose argent. The rose appears on each side of the crowned head, and in the four angles of the cross on the reverse of the silver money.[12]

The representatives of the people agreed to pay a tax, called *fogatje*, for the support of the mint, assessed on all houses having hearths.

A pure currency is a great aid to commerce, and the trade of Majorca increased rapidly under the auspices of En Jayme. Shipbuilding progressed, and the rich and fertile soil began to yield abundant crops. The cultivation of olive-trees, though many of them now present such an extraordinarily antiquated appearance, was introduced into the island by the Catalans, and not by the Arabs.[13] The raising of stock also received much attention from the King, who in this as in other measures for the prosperity of the island, was well supported by his 'Ricos hombres.'

The 'Almudaina,' or alcazar of the Moors, is a huge bastille on the right of the landing-place. The lofty walls still stand, enclosing a large space, with square towers at intervals. The exterior has undergone considerable modern alterations, but it is still quite easy to make out the appearance of the original building. King Jayme II. brought artists and expert artificers from Perpignan to convert this ancient alcazar of the Almudaina into a palace. The royal apartments were decorated with paintings and bas-reliefs, the beautiful oratory of Santa Ana was built as the royal chapel, pleasant balconies were erected, and gardens were laid out in the courts and on the terraces. The sculptor François Camprodon was employed to adorn the halls and gardens with statues. A code of palace etiquette was drawn up, and the Majorcan Court was ceremoniously conducted, while at the same time it was a home of pleasure and festivity.

To the east of the Almudaina there was a space, said to have been occupied by a garden in Moorish times, on a high platform overlooking the Mediterranean. No finer site could be found for a cathedral. The Capilla Real had been finished in the time of the Conqueror, but during the usurpation work had been stopped. Funds were raised under Jayme II. and the construction of this beautiful edifice was continued. All the stone came from the quarries of Santañi, on the south coast of the island. The cathedral presents rather a curious appearance from the sea, owing to the crowd of flying buttresses and the absence of windows, which are only allowed to give full light through stained glass in the apse. The nave is very lofty, with eight arches on each side, between seven high and slender pillars supporting a finely vaulted roof. There is a clerestory with windows blocked, but no triforium. The aisles are lower and rather narrow, with side chapels. The lofty and slender pillars rising to the vault, less than three feet in diameter, give a peculiarly solemn effect which is alike pleasing and imposing.[14] The Bishop's palace, built round a courtyard, is to the east of the cathedral, and also overlooks the sea.

The King's eldest son had devoted his life to religion and had become a Franciscan monk. Out of affection for him Jayme II. founded a large Franciscan monastery. A fine church rose up in due time, with a very picturesque cloister of two storeys, other buildings used as schools, and a large library with a richly carved wooden ceiling. All came to ruin on the expulsion of the monks in 1835.

En Jayme also planned and commenced one of the finest military works of his time. The castle of Belver is a beautiful object from the sea, standing on the summit of a pine-clad hill, with a background of more distant mountains. It is elliptical in shape, with a large courtyard in the centre. The accommodation is spacious. On the ground floor there is a series of vaulted chambers suitable for barracks, guard rooms, or prisons. Above there is a vaulted gallery opening on numerous large rooms, also vaulted, including a large hall and a chapel. The roof is flat and paved. Standing by itself there is a tall tower, called 'el Torre de Homenaje,' connected with the roof by an arch. The whole is surrounded by a deep moat. Pedro Salva, the architect, was a native of Majorca. The hill on which the castle stands, 450 feet above the sea, is entirely covered with pine-trees (*Pinus Halepensis*), with an undergrowth of *lentisco*-bushes, wild lavender, and a purple cistus. Between the bushes the ground is covered with asphodel and the leaves of an arisarum.

En Jayme brought architects, sculptors, and decorators to Majorca, as well as troubadours and musicians, and he encouraged native talent. But the great ornament of his reign was an eminent philosopher and theologian. Ramon Lull, or Raimundo Lulio of Barcelona, was one of the companions of Jayme I., and received two *alquerias* or farms at the partition. He was married to Heril de Cataluña, and their son Raimundo was born in the capital of Majorca in about the year 1235. His parents wished him to learn to read, but he cared for nothing but arms, and became a page to En Jayme. He neglected his duties to the Prince and gave up nearly all his time to rather scandalous love affairs. His parents thought that the only cure was marriage, and they married him to a girl named Catalina Labots; but this only appeared to increase his devotion to other married women. His conversion was miraculous. He had a celestial vision in the garden of the bishop's palace, and another in his own house, when he heard the words, 'Raimundo, follow me!' He sold all his property, only reserving a small portion for his wife and children, and in 1266 he embarked for Barcelona to visit the shrines of Montserrat and Santiago. He then returned home to cause edification by his example in the same place where his former life had been so scandalous. He was well past his thirtieth year.

Lulio then began to learn Arabic from a slave, with the intention of preaching to the Moors; but one day he flogged his teacher for blaspheming God, who retaliated by stabbing Lulio in the breast. The new convert then left the abodes of man and went up an isolated hill called Randa, well in sight from the anchorage off the capital of Majorca. Here his life was a continual succession of prayers, penitence, and tears. He was favoured with more celestial visions. His mind seems to have been filled with zeal for the conversion of unbelievers; and he also developed some crude philosophical ideas in his solitude. Jayme II. was at this time at Montpellier, and, hearing of the miraculous conversion of his former page, he sent for him. En Jayme was struck by the earnestness, the eloquence, and the ability of the new convert. When Lulio entreated the King to establish a school in Majorca for teaching Arabic, with a view to preaching to the infidels, he consented. He made a grant of money sufficient to sustain thirteen monks, and assigned for their college a farm in a lovely spot on the north coast of the island, overlooking the sea, called Miramar. Here Lulio studied, and wrote his theories and ideas; but his plan did not succeed, and the college was a failure.

Lulio went to Rome, and then to Paris, where he read his system and argued some points with the famous Duns Scotus and his disciples. In 1290 he was at Montpellier and Genoa, whence he embarked for Tunis. Here he preached the faith of Christ openly, was beaten, and eventually banished. He travelled through Armenia and the holy Land; and afterwards wandered over Europe, preaching a crusade to recover Jerusalem. Another year found him at Paris once more, reading his system, which at length received the approbation of the University. In 1314 Lulio was again travelling through Egypt and the Holy Land; and two years afterwards we find him in England, studying physics as then understood. During the intervals of travel he diligently wrote books on every imaginable subject. He reached his eightieth year, and longed for martyrdom. So he embarked in a vessel bound for Tunis, and went thence to Bugia. He preached Christ openly and persistently until he was taken out of the town and stoned. Some Genoese begged for the martyr's body, and conveyed it to Majorca. The date of the martyrdom was June 29, 1315. Lulio was buried in the church of San Francisco. The effigy of the martyr rests sideways and rather high up on the wall of a transept; above it two angels are bearing up his soul, below are the arms of Lulio and Majorca, at the sides angels in niches.

The philosophy of Lulio is part of the intellectual history of his century, and can have no place here; but this meagre sketch of his life and acts is sufficient to show that he was one of the most remarkable men of his time. Majorca has good reason to be proud of him. His works were read and taught in the Franciscan monastery and elsewhere, and his statue at Palma is a sufficient proof of the appreciation of his countrymen.

Raimundo Lulio survived his old master by four years. Jayme II. continued to maintain an excellent understanding with his nephew and namesake of Aragon, affording him assistance in ships and men in his conquest of Corsica and Sardinia. He died in his palace of Almudaina on May 28, 1371, and was succeeded by his second son, Sancho. Among many adherents, his most faithful friend through all his troubles was his secretary, Guillermo de Puigdorfila. This noble Majorcan was possessed of a large fortune, which he devoted to the service of his master, and was his most trusted councillor to the last. His descendants continued to flourish in Majorca for 540 years, the last male dying in 1846.

Jayme II. was buried in the Royal chapel of the cathedral at Majorca, and in 1779 Charles III. of Spain erected a monument to his memory, in doubtful taste. On a parchment at the lid of the shroud it is recorded that: 'Here is Jayme (Jacma) of worthy memory, King of Majorca, Count of Roussillon and Cerdaña, Lord of Montpellier, who departed this life in this city on the 28th of May, vigil of Pentecost, 1311, son of en Jayme, King of Aragon, who delivered this city from the heathens.' The body is well preserved as a mummy. Jayme II. of Majorca was an excellent king for peaceful times, and in the last fifteen years of his life his administration was most useful and serviceable to his country.

CHAPTER IX
THE CAREER OF PRINCE FERNANDO OF MAJORCA; AND TELLS HOW THE ORPHAN WAS TAKEN HOME TO ITS GRANDMOTHER

Fernando, the third son of King Jayme II. of Majorca, was a splendid type of a chivalrous knight, trained to arms from early youth, eager to win renown, but placing honour and his word before all earthly considerations. He was very young when he left his home in Majorca to fight for his gallant cousin, Federigo of Sicily. After the peace with Naples, Fernando still remained with his cousin. Then news came of the murder of Friar Roger de Flor, and of the critical position of the Catalan company at Gallipoli, which place they had held for several years, making occasional raids into Roumania. The King of Sicily proposed to his cousin Fernando that he should assume command of the company in the name of Federigo as overlord. Fernando accepted the charge. He arrived at Gallipoli with four galleys, and announced that he came only as lieutenant and representative of the King of Sicily. Ramon Muntaner, our worthy chronicler, who was in charge at Gallipoli, received the young Prince in the capacity announced in the diplomas he brought from King Federigo as chief and commander of the company. En Rocafort, with the greater part of the forces, was besieging a town called Nona, sixty miles from Gallipoli, and he requested the Prince to join him. The other two chiefs of the company, En Berenguer de Entenza and En Ferrar Ximenes, remained at Gallipoli; but the Prince, with Muntaner, proceeded to Nona, where he was received with great honour. Rocafort was at enmity with Entenza and Ximenes, and secretly wished to get rid of the Prince so as to have sole command of the company. He therefore intrigued with all the chiefs and officers, persuading them to accept the Prince as their lord, but not as a representative of the King of Sicily. They all agreed, and Rocafort knew what the Prince's answer, as a man of honour, must necessarily be. When the Prince announced his decision, he was entreated to remain until they reached Salonica, to which place the company intended to march, it being represented to him that he might compose the differences between Rocafort and the other leaders. The Prince consented to remain with them for a short time with that object.

Gallipoli was to be abandoned, and the duty of destroying the castle there and bringing away the wives and children of the company was entrusted to Muntaner. He did this, and brought the people to Cristopol, at the entrance of the Salonica territory, in thirty-six vessels, consisting of galleys, armed *leños*, and armed boats.

The whole company, including Entenza and Ximenes with their troops, then began their march to Salonica. On the second day there was an affray in which Entenza was killed, Rocafort pretending that his men mistook Entenza's men for enemies. Ximenes fled. The Prince, who now saw through the designs of Rocafort, was in a very difficult position, when his four galleys most opportunely arrived at the part of the coast where the company was encamped. A council was called, and the Prince told Rocafort and his party plainly that if they would not receive him as vicegerent of the King of Sicily, he would leave them. Rocafort induced the leaders to declare that they would receive him only as their lord, independent of any one else. Prince Fernando therefore embarked and went with his four galleys to the island of Thasos.

Rocafort's ambition led to his ruin, for his own people became tired of his tyranny and greed. He wanted to make himself King of Salonica, but there was a mutiny; he was delivered over to the commander of some Venetian galleys and taken to Naples with his brother. The Venetians gave him up to King Robert of Naples, who put him and his brother into a dungeon in the castle of Aversa, where they were left to die of starvation. The company took service under the French Duke of Athens.

Thasos is by far the most beautiful island in the Archipelago. It has pleasant meads, wooded glens, and picturesque mountain scenery. There are many remains of ancient Greece, and on a green hill rise the ruins of a fine old castle built by the Genoese. In this delightful retreat Prince Fernando rested for a few days after the troubles and anxieties caused by his brief connection with the company. He was joined by Ramon Muntaner with his followers, who was devoted to the House of Aragon.

In returning to Sicily they were attacked off Negropont by a superior force of Venetians, and the Prince was taken prisoner. He was delivered over to King Robert of Naples, who kept him in captivity until, through the intervention of the King of France, he was allowed to return to his home in Majorca.

The next enterprise in which Prince Fernando was engaged was against the Moors of Granada. The King of Aragon agreed with Fernando IV. ('the Summoned'[15]) of Castille to carry on this war from two different directions. One was to attack Almeria, while the other besieged Algesiras, and there was a promise that neither should retire without the consent of the other. The object was to divide the Moslem forces. The Prince of Majorca went with his cousin of Aragon to the siege of Almeria. This seaport town, very beautifully situated at the entrance of a fertile valley backed by mountains, was a place of great commercial importance in the days of the Beni Omeyya Khâlifas, and here they had their naval dockyard. Almeria continued to flourish under the Kings of Granada, and at one time it had kings of its own. The siege lasted for nine months, and the Aragonese brought with them all the artillery of the day to batter the walls. Prince Fernando was well fitted out by his father. He had under his command a hundred Majorcan knights, many foot soldiers, with galleys and *leños* to convey the horses, provisions, and artillery. During the siege Fernando proved himself to be a good knight by his valorous deeds—'One of the best knights in the world,' Muntaner says. Among other combats, he had three hand-to-hand fights with Moorish warriors, and won the palm of a good knight in each encounter, in sight of both armies.

Fernando IV. (the Summoned One) broke his word, raised the siege of Algesiras, and retreated. This liberated a large Moorish force, which was at once sent to Almeria. It was done without informing the King of Aragon, who suddenly found himself confronted by the whole power of Granada. On the eve of St. Bartholomew a great Moorish army suddenly attacked the besiegers. The King of Aragon was surprised, but not dismayed. He ordered Prince Fernando to remain near the town with his contingent, at a place called the 'Esperonte'[16] of Almeria, to attack and drive back the besieged, if they sallied out to fall upon the Aragonese rear while they were engaged with the Moorish army in front. This was a most honourable post, and Fernando held it gallantly. The 'Esperonte' faced the seashore. While the battle was raging a son of the Moorish King of Guadix sallied forth at the head of a large force with loud shouts and war-cries. Fernando was well prepared. His men were formed to resist attack. The Moor was one of the most famous warriors of Granada. He was well in front, scimitar in hand, shouting, 'Ani ibn es-Sultan.' 'What does he say?' asked Fernando. 'He says that he is the King's son,' replied the interpreter. 'If he is a King's son, so am I,' answered the Prince; and, putting spurs to his horse, he attacked the Moor. Before he could reach him he had killed six of the enemy with his own hand, breaking his lance on the sixth. He then drew his sword and closed with the Moorish King's son. The Moor struck such a wonderful blow that he cut off a quarter of the Prince's shield, and again shouted 'Ani ibn es-Sultan.' But the Prince delivered such a blow that he cut open the Moor's head down to his teeth, and he fell dead. His followers were routed, and few escaped back into the town.

Meanwhile the great Moorish army was entirely defeated. The King of Aragon returned victorious to his tent, to hear of the great service performed by his cousin and of his deeds of derring-do, equalling, says Muntaner, those of the famous Roland. The King then raised the siege and returned to Barcelona for three reasons. The winter was approaching, the Castillian King had broken faith, and he of Aragon had gained a greater success by the liberation of many Christian captives which he made a condition of his truce, than if he had taken Almeria. Prince Fernando joined his father and mother at Perpignan, who rejoiced at his safe return.

En Fernando remained at home until he heard that Robert of Naples, who had married his sister Sancha, was making war on the King of Sicily. Ever true to his cousin En Federigo, the young Prince assembled his knightly followers, and, with a good contingent of Majorcans, he joined his cousin of Sicily. En Federigo was delighted to see him, for they had not met since En Fernando set out to join the company. The King granted the Majorcan prince the city of Catania for his life, and two thousand *onzas* a year from his treasury. The cousins lived very happily together until King Robert of Naples landed an army at Palermo and besieged Trapani. Prince Fernando was sent to occupy Mount St. Julian, where once stood the famous temple of Venus, whence his *almogavares* gave a very bad time to the besieging host. The King of Sicily fitted out a large fleet of galleys to prevent any escape, and then joined Prince Fernando on Mount St. Julian, to attack the besiegers with a superior force. At this critical juncture the Dowager Queen of Naples, sister of Jayme II. of Aragon, intervened, and a truce was arranged, Robert of Naples surrendering all he had gained and evacuating Sicily.

During the rest of his life Prince Fernando was connected with the affairs of Greece. Long before, the Duke of Burgundy and the Comte de la Marche, grandsons of the King of France, had invaded the Morea, driven out the Grecian rulers, founded the city of Patras, and established the French dukedom of Athens and principality of the Morea. The Catalan company finally put an end to the Athens dukedom by killing the Comte de Brienne and all his nobles. In the Morea, Louis, the fifth in descent from the Duke of Burgundy, died without male heirs, but left two daughters. One inherited the Morea, and the other the Barony of Matagrifon. One was married to Felipe, a younger son of Charles of Anjou, and the other to his friend the Count of Andria. Felipe was recognised as Prince of the Morea, and his friend as Baron of Matagrifon. Philip died childless, and his widow married a Comte de Nevers. The Count of Andria died, leaving a daughter Isabel, who was unjustly deprived of her inheritance. Her mother thought that there was no knight in Christendom who would be more likely to take up the cause of an injured and dispossessed princess than En Fernando of Majorca.

The mother, with her beautiful daughter, came to Messina, where they were hospitably received by the King of Sicily. Muntaner says that Isabel was the fairest, the rosiest, the most discreet maiden he had ever seen. The marriage of En Fernando with the fair Isabel of Andria took place at Messina, and, after several days of festivity, the Prince took his bride to Catania. Muntaner was then in command of the island of Gerbes, on the African coast, but he at once complied with a request that he should join En

Fernando. He arrived at Catania a few days before the Princess gave birth to a fine boy. He brought with him great store of wedding presents, consisting of richly embroidered dresses, slippers of finely dressed leather, cloth of various colours, and jewels. He spread them all out before the Prince and Princess, to their great delight. The birthday was on the first Saturday in April 1315. The child received the name of Jayme in the cathedral of St. Agatha at Catania.

There was a melancholy termination to the bright prospect which seemed to open before the young married pair. En Fernando had no sooner completed his preparations to sail for the Morea with a well-equipped force and recover his wife's dominions, than Isabel was seized with a fever and died a month after the birth of her child. She died in her husband's arms, who was thus plunged in grief and was long inconsolable. He buried his bride under a monument near the tomb of St. Agatha.

In sorrow the bereaved Prince commenced his campaign. He was joined at Messina by the faithful Ramon Muntaner, whose guidance as a chronicler we are soon to lose. He had been governor of the Isle of Gerbes for seven years, but resigned that important appointment to share the fortunes of his beloved Prince. En Fernando told Muntaner that he owed more to him than to any other man on earth; but that he was now going to ask him the greatest favour of all. The little child at Catania was most in need of a valiant defender. The Prince entreated Muntaner to give up the campaign in the Morea and to convey his motherless boy safely to its grandmother at Perpignan. He would have letters to her, to the King of Majorca, and to the Prince's procurator, En Berenguer Despuig, and he would be supplied with well-fitted galleys for the voyage. With a heavy heart Muntaner undertook the charge, and took leave of the Prince who had won his devoted affection.

Prince Fernando then made sail for the Morea with a strong force of cavalry and of *almogavares*. He landed near Clarencia, a small seaport on the coast, south-west of Patras, and, after a feeble resistance, captured the town. The people swore allegiance to him, for Clarencia was part of his wife's inheritance. He then proceeded with the conquest of the rest of the Morea, and when he seemed well established he sent envoys to the King of Cyprus, asking for the hand of his niece Isabella. The marriage took place at Clarencia, and there was a son, named Fernando, born after his father's death.

Louis of Burgundy, who had married Mahault of Hainault, Princess of Achaia, set out to dispute the possession of the Morea with Prince Fernando in 1315. Landing at Patras, he advanced towards Clarencia, and Fernando came out to meet him. There was a battle at a place called Esfero on July 7, 1316, when the gallant young Prince was slain. He had sent for reinforcements, but his impetuosity prevented him from waiting for them.

Muntaner received the sad news in Majorca, and declared that this was the greatest loss the House of Aragon had ever sustained. 'For,' he added, 'this was the best and most valiant knight to be found among the sons of kings in that age, the most just, and the one who best knew how to order his actions.' The body was conveyed to Perpignan, and arrived just after his mother's death. The widow returned to Cyprus, where her child was born.

But we must return to the orphan boy at Catania. Having selected a galley of Barcelona for the voyage, Muntaner chose an excellent person as head nurse, a native of the Ampurdan, named Na Ines de Adri, who was experienced in nursing, having had twenty-two children herself. He also engaged a very robust young woman of Catania as wet-nurse, and several maids. These particulars are mentioned to show with what care the old soldier entered upon his new duties. He took with him attested proofs signed by those who were present at the birth and baptism. On the day appointed for sailing Muntaner left the city with the infant in his arms, followed by more than two thousand people. As he was embarking, a messenger arrived from King Federigo with two dresses of cloth of gold as a present to his little cousin. On August 1, 1315, Muntaner made sail from Catania. On arriving at Trapani he received tidings that four galleys were waiting for him, to seize the infant and thus dispose of the heir to Clarencia and Matagrifon. Muntaner therefore took more armed men on board and waited to join a fleet of twenty-four Catalan vessels. He then put to sea. After a few days a storm raged so furiously that seven ships sank and the rest were in great danger. At length he let go his anchor in the port of Salou. The child had never been out of his arms during the whole time that the storm lasted, either by night or day, the nurse being dreadfully seasick; nor could any of the other women stand on their legs.

En Pedro de Rocaberti, the Archbishop of Tarragona, sent good horses to Salou, and the party went by easy stages to Barcelona, where the King of Aragon received them with much hospitality, kissing and blessing the little child. Muntaner caused a litter to be made at Barcelona for the nurse and child, which was borne on the shoulders of twenty men; and so by very easy stages they reached Perpignan in twenty-four days. They proceeded to the castle, where the Queens of Majorca then resided. When they reached the gates Muntaner took the child in his own arms and with great joy brought it into the presence of its grandmother, who, with its aunt-in-law, the reigning Queen, was seated to receive it. 'God,' he exclaims, 'does not give a greater joy than that which my lady the Queen, its grandmother, then felt on seeing the child so well nurtured, with its face wreathed with smiles, and its body wrapped in cloth of gold.' Muntaner knelt and kissed the hands of the two Queens, making the child do the same. He declared that this was the infant Jayme, son of the Prince En Fernando and of Isabel his wife. Its grandmother then took it in her arms and kissed it many times.

Soon afterwards the King of Majorca, who had been in France, arrived at Perpignan, and very joyfully received his nephew, making all the usual rules and regulations for his being brought up as if he was his own son.

It must have been a great relief to En Ramon Muntaner to have performed this last and most responsible duty for his beloved Prince. He had been recruiting for him in Valencia and was in Majorca, preparing to join him, when the sad news of his death arrived. The kind old grandmother, En Fernando's mother, Esclaramunda de Foix, died in the sane year. Alas! the good Muntaner had preserved a life destined in the years to come to more than the usual share of sorrow, misfortune, and disaster. The child became the unhappy Jayme III., last reigning King of Majorca, Count of Roussillon, Cerdaña, and Conflent, and Lord of Montpellier. He was also Lord of Clarencia in the Morea and of Matagrifon.

Besides little Jayme, Prince Fernando had three illegitimate sons, named Fernando, Pagano, and Sancho. They came to Majorca, and were ever the loyal and devoted brothers and friends of their young master Jayme, in prosperity and in adversity.

CHAPTER X
KING SANCHO OF MAJORCA

Sancho, the second son of Jayme II., succeeded as King of Majorca on June 4, 1311. He was a just and peace-loving sovereign, beloved by his people, always on excellent terms with his cousins of Aragon, and he reigned prosperously for thirteen years. Majorca was a feudatory of Aragon, with the duty of assisting in the wars of the suzerain; and the King was required to attend the Cortes of the Aragonese kingdom to arrange the nature and amount of aid to be contributed to the feudal overlord.

As a boy Sancho had suffered imprisonment with his brothers Felipe and Fernando, when they were captured by the young tyrant Alfonso III., first at Torrella de Monguin, then at Gerona, and finally at Barcelona, where they were released on Alfonso's death. The misfortunes of his boyhood were not continued in after-life. His reign was prosperous. On his accession he swore to maintain the privileges and freedom of his people; and the commerce of the island made great progress under his fostering care.

Sancho married Maria, daughter of the Angevin King of Naples, but had no children by her. They both adopted the infant son of the chivalrous younger brother Fernando. The King of Majorca was in a position calling for much tact and diplomatic skill on the one hand, and for energetic defensive measures on the other. He had to be well prepared against attacks of pirates from the coasts of Barbary, to preserve his Continental dominions from French encroachments, and to maintain a good understanding with his cousin of Aragon.

A fleet of armed ships was equipped for defence against piratical attacks, half by the King and half by the Jurados. It consisted of four galleys, two galleots, and several smaller vessels. Later, the *atalayas*, or watch-towers, were built along the coasts, which gave notice of the approach of an enemy by fire-signals. In 1316 King Sancho proceeded from Perpignan to Avignon for an interview with the Pope respecting French claims on the Barony of Montpellier. The negotiations were transferred to Paris, and a satisfactory settlement was arrived at. With Aragon Sancho continued to maintain the most friendly relations. When the conquest of Sardinia and Corsica was resolved to be undertaken, he attended personally at the Cortes held at Gerona in June 1322 as a feudatory of Aragon. The result was that Majorca contributed twenty new galleys to the expedition, two hundred mounted knights, besides a contingent of foot soldiers. King Jayme II. of Aragon was so much pleased with this evidence of good will on the part of his cousin of Majorca that he expressed his satisfaction by exempting King Sancho from the duty of personal attendance at the Cortes of Aragon.

King Sancho built a castle for his residence in the lovely ravine of Valdemosa, in the mountains on the north-west coast, to the west of Soller. From Palma the way is across the fertile *huerta*, or garden, for eight miles, when the hilly region is entered. There is terraced cultivation up the mountain-sides with orange-trees and olives; higher up, woods of Aleppo pines; and above them the marble cliffs rise perpendicularly, their irregular outline standing out against the blue sky. The castle stood across the highest part of the pass, a picturesque line of masonry rising from the groves of orange and lemon trees. The first Alcaide, or Castellan, of the castle of Valdemosa was Martin de Muntaner, a relation of the chronicler. Here King Sancho held his court, and here he enjoyed hawking and other sports of the field. He had a special breed of falcons, which was famous all over Europe, and he introduced partridges into the island. Beyond Valdemosa the scenery increases in beauty as the sea on the north side of the island comes in sight. Here was the college founded by Jayme II. at the request of Raimundo Lulio, but soon abandoned. King Sancho suffered from asthma, and he found relief in the climate of Miramar, passing much time in the building which had been erected for an Arabic college. Far below is the sea, the steep slopes descending to it being covered with flowering shrubs and Aleppo pines, while behind the marble cliffs shoot up into peaks and ridges. His infirmity increasing, Sancho was advised to try the climate of his Continental dominions. The heat was very great in the summer of 1324, and he retired to the cooler air of the Pyrenees. There he died in the little village of Santa Maria de Formiguera, in the county of Cerdaña, on September 4, 1324. The King's body was conveyed to Perpignan, where it was interred in the church of San Juan.

Sancho left a will in the custody of his friend Bernardo Truyolls. In it he declared his infant nephew Jayme to be his heir, and appointed his brother, the priest Felipe, to be Regent during the minority. His widow, daughter of Charles II. of Naples, married secondly Jayme, Lord of Ezerica, son of another Jayme, the illegitimate son of Jayme I. (the Conqueror).

Sancho was a wise and just sovereign, and secured a period of peace and prosperity for the islands and the islanders he loved so well.

There is a very rare gold coin of King Sancho, a two-real piece, and a *dobler de potin*, the two latter resembling those of Jayme II.

CHAPTER XI
KING JAYME III. OF MAJORCA

The little child who was brought home with such care and through so many dangers from Catania now succeeded his uncle Sancho as Jayme III., King of Majorca, Count of Roussillon, Conflent, and Cerdaña, Lord of Montpellier, and, in his own right, as the heir of his mother, Lord of Clarencia in the Morea[17] and of Matagrifon.

Jayme had a happy childhood, and there was no premonition of the sorrows and calamities of his after-life. His clerical uncle Felipe was accepted as Regent by the Ricos Hombres of Majorca and the Cortes of Aragon, and, after some demur, by Roussillon and Cerdaña. The young King received a good education under the supervision of En Felipe, and was brought up with his elder half-brothers Fernando, Pagano, and Sancho, who trained him in martial exercises. Among his dearest friends was Arnaldo de Santa Cilia. This noble and loyal Majorcan was the son of Pedro Juan Santa Cilia, a knight of the conquest, whose original home was a castle of the same name on the banks of the river Ter, near Vich in Catalonia. Pedro Juan married Leonor Ben-nasser, the baptized heiress of the Arab chief Benahabet, who helped King Jayme in the conquest. Through her the Santa Cilias became the owners of the beautiful country seat of Alfavia.

The Regent Philip continued the wise policy of his brother. He took the boy King to Barcelona to do homage to King Jayme II. of Aragon, and furnished a strong contingent to his suzerain for the Sardinian war. He also negotiated a marriage between Jayme III. of Majorca and Constance, the young granddaughter of the King of Aragon, daughter of his heir Alfonso (who succeeded as Alfonso IV. in 1327) by Teresa de Entensa of Urgel.

Jayme III. was an amiable and gallant prince, always loyal and correct in all his dealings with his suzerain and beloved by his subjects. Of his elder half-brothers, Fernando appears to have retired to Italy. But Pagano and Sancho were his tutors in arms, counsellors, staunch and loyal friends through life. Pagano was married to Blanca, daughter of Ramon Sabellos, and Sancho to Sauria, daughter of Ferrario Rossello.

All went well until the accession, in 1335, of Pedro IV., son of Alfonso IV. and brother of Constance, the wife of Jayme III. of Majorca. She had another brother, Jayme, Count of Urgel, a far better man. Pedro was an odious character. Jayme III. came to Barcelona with his wife Constance, and did homage to his brother-in-law for his Balearic and Continental dominions, proceeding thence to Perpignan. There he was joined by Pedro, and the two Kings went together to Avignon—Pedro to do homage to the Pope for the new conquests of Sardinia and Corsica.

On his return to Aragon Pedro soon began to show himself in his true character. From the first he coveted the Balearic Islands, and resolved to seize them in defiance of right and justice. With such a man, a hatred of his unfortunate brother-in-law and cousin, who stood in the way of his ambition, was the inevitable consequence of his greed.

Pedro IV. combined the evil qualities of our two Henry Tudors. He had all the avarice and cunning meanness of the father and the heartless cruelty of the son, together with his love of display and magnificence. Hence he was called 'Pedro the Ceremonious.' He soon began to seek for excuses for his contemplated usurpation. His first accusation was that the King of Majorca allowed French money to circulate in his Continental dominions, which he alleged to be derogatory to his suzerainty. He then wrote letters to the Jurados of Majorca, accusing their King of contumacy. Their reply was that their King had done nothing opposed to the dignity, honour, or rights of the King of Aragon; but, on the contrary, that he had complied with all his obligations loyally and faithfully, and that they would stand by him as devoted subjects. This reply was dated June 18, 1342.

Jayme III. had returned to Majorca, and his son, also named Jayme, was born in the Almudaina in 1334. Isabel, his daughter, followed in 1338, just when the dark clouds were gathering around their father's horizon.

Pedro found that the accusation about the currency was absurd and untenable. He therefore deliberately concocted an infamous lie, declaring that his brother-in-law intended to kidnap him at Barcelona and carry him off to a dungeon in Majorca. He added that God, Who never failed those that trusted in Him, had, by reason of the piety and goodness of the Ceremonious one, disclosed the treason.

A fleet was prepared at Barcelona for the conquest of Majorca, and on February 21, 1343, Pedro published what he called the sentence, declaring the King of Majorca to be contumacious and guilty of treason against his suzerain, and that he was therefore deprived of all his dominions. Jayme III., through his procurator Pedro Pascual, published a complete refutation of the false statements in the so-called sentence, and a well-reasoned proof of his rights. Pedro's aunt Sancha, the Queen of Naples, entreated him to refrain from hostilities and to let the questions be settled by arbitration.

All was of no avail. On May 10, 1343, Pedro embarked with 110 sail of vessels, 29 being war-galleys, arriving on the coast of the island on the 23rd. King Jayme had hastily collected some troops to resist this unjust invasion. But they were quickly routed by the vastly superior force of the invaders, and the unfortunate King took ship and retired to Perpignan. There was a great slaughter, and the city had no alternative but submission. The usurper entered in triumph, declaring Majorca and its dependent islands to be annexed to the crown of Aragon. Nicolas de Marin, the loyal castellan of Belver, held out for a short time, but he was forced to capitulate. A cruel persecution of all the friends of the King of Majorca was then commenced. The Queen and her two children were captured, and kept in close imprisonment at Barcelona.

In July Pedro returned from Majorca, assembled troops at Gerona, and prepared to attack his brother-in-law's Continental dominions. He advanced to Figueras, where he received a letter from the unfortunate Jayme asking for an interview. The only reply was a threat that Perpignan should be destroyed. But the town was faithful, though Jayme was scarcely able to maintain the troops that remained loyal to him. At last, in January 1344, poor Jayme humbled himself to the extent of entreating mercy from his coldblooded and relentless brother-in-law. He submitted entirely, in the hope of some feeling of generosity or pity on the part of the usurper of his dominions. But of any such feeling the Ceremonious one was quite incapable. He seized upon Perpignan, and sent the King of Majorca to Berga, where he was offered a pension on condition that he abandoned all his rights of every description. The object of Pedro was to drive his brother-in-law to despair and exterminate his family.

Jayme was indeed in despair. His wife, in spite of her entreaties, was not allowed by her unfeeling brother to join him. But the imprisonment of the two innocent children was more than some noble Catalans could stand. They broke into the prison, killed the jailer, and contrived that Prince Jayme and his sister should escape to their father. At the same time there was a revulsion of feeling in favour of the persecuted King. The French Court interceded in his favour, and he received letters and messages from Majorca inviting him to return. He still retained the Barony of Montpellier. He sold it to King Philip of France for 120,000 *escudos de oro*, with which he raised troops and equipped vessels for the invasion of Majorca. The King of France and the Queen of Sicily assisted him, especially with ships. King Jayme collected eight galleys and many smaller vessels, on board of which he embarked 3,000 infantry and 400 cavalry. His half-brothers, Pagano and Sancho, faithful to the end, were with him. There, too, was his young son Jayme, just escaped from the dungeon at Barcelona. Carlos de Grimaldi, of the noble Genoese family, was one of his chief commanders. He had been granted the towns of Soller and Alcudia, while his brother Ayto was to have the estate of Buñola, both with the title of Count. Thus the ill-fated King sailed from the coast of Provence on his last disastrous attempt to regain his kingdom.

En Gilabert de Centelles was then Governor of Majorca for the usurper, and he had a large force under his command. King Jayme landed with his little army on the south coast of the island, and advanced with some hope of success. But Centelles had an overwhelmingly superior force of 20,000 infantry and 800 cavalry. The hostile armies met near the town of Lluchmayor, to the south-east of Palma. The King led a small squadron of cavalry and some French infantry in the van, and was the first to encounter the enemy. But there was a panic, and his troops fled in confusion. With only a few faithful knights he fought valorously until, covered with wounds, he fell from his horse. When on the ground a brutal soldier cut off his head. He had reigned for twenty-five years, from 1324 to 1349, the first eleven years happily and in peace, the last fourteen bowed down by calamity and sorrow. Jayme III. was a prince of many virtues. He was conscientiously religious, well versed in the learning of his time, animated and eloquent, and devoted to the interests of his subjects. His wife Constance was faithful to him throughout his misfortunes, though long separated from him by the heartless cruelty of her brother. His young son loved him with a passionate fondness, which led to his giving up his whole life to avenge his father's death. His half-brothers fought by his side at Lluchmayor, and their wives were thrown into prison. Sancho, the youngest, lead a daughter named Esclaramunda, who married Antal, Count of Foix, and was buried in the cathedral of Palma.

For more than a hundred years the Aragonese Kings of Majorca had ruled over the islands well and prosperously and to the great good of the inhabitants. They were an exceptionally noble and high-souled race, worthy of their descent from the 'great Conquistador.'

The body of Jayme III. is said to have been buried at Valencia. Born at Catania on April 5, 1315, his age was thirty-four and some months. The fatal battle of Lluchmayor was on August 25, 1349.

CHAPTER XII
RELATES THE ADVENTURES OF JAYME AND ISABEL, DESCRIBES THE MEMORIAL CHAIR, AND RECORDS THE END OF THE MAJORCAN DYNASTY

Never did sovereign ascend a throne under such appalling circumstances as did Jayme IV., the last King of Majorca. The young Prince was little more than fifteen years of age, yet he fought by his father's side and was severely wounded. He was carried to Belver Castle by the side of his father's corpse. As soon as he was well enough to be moved, he was again taken to Barcelona and thrown into prison, where his uncle, the Ceremonious one, intended him to rot and die. The intercessions of his relations and of the Pope were all useless.

There were people in Catalonia to whom this tormenting of children was hateful and intolerable. The escape was no easy task. The guards were carefully chosen, and changed every week. The prison was a disgrace to Pedro IV. as a place for the confinement of an innocent relation. The boy had to sleep in a sort of iron cage, and the guards never left him by night or day. Jayme de San Clemente, an official of the cathedral, was shocked at the treatment of the young Prince. He and a few friends succeeded in getting impressions of the keys of the castle doors and in making false ones; and they had the aid of some merciful officials within. The rescuers killed Nicolas Rovira, the captain of the guard, and liberated the prisoner, who escaped out of Barcelona. It does not appear where he was during the next two or three years, but probably in some safe refuge with his mother and sister. The brother and sister were devoted to each other.

In 1362, the year when her second husband died, a handsome youth appeared at the court of Queen Juana of Naples. She fell in love with him, and they were married in the same year. This was Jayme IV., King of Majorca, who thus became also King of Naples. Juana committed many crimes, especially as regards her first husband; but all may be condoned in consideration of her unchanging loyalty and generosity to young Jayme. The exiled King told his wife from the first that his life must be devoted to the recovery of his dominions and to avenge the cruel treatment of his father. With these objects he opened communications with Pedro of Castille, who was at enmity with his namesake, the Ceremonious one of Aragon. Jayme, supported by funds supplied by his Queen, joined the Black Prince, and distinguished himself by his valour in the battle of Najara.

Soon afterwards the cause of Pedro of Castille became hopeless. His illegitimate brother Henry of Trastamara, aided by the Ceremonious tyrant of Aragon, advanced into Spain with an army and besieged the castle of Burgos, which had been occupied by Jayme and his troops. The King of Majorca made a gallant defence, but at last he was obliged to surrender. His odious uncle of Aragon tried to get his unfortunate nephew into his clutches again; but love was ready to make greater sacrifices than hatred. The Queen of Naples ransomed her husband for sixty thousand *doblas*.

In March 1369 Jayme was safe in the territory of the Count of Foix. Thence he proceeded to Avignon and began to collect troops, intending to invade Roussillon, which had been unjustly occupied by the usurper. His whole heart was devoted to what he considered the duty of avenging his father's death. He looked upon his uncle Pedro as a usurper and murderer, and his hatred for the Ceremonious one was intense. Friends represented to him that he should be satisfied with the kingdom of Naples and a devoted wife. But he answered that he was bound to avenge his father. When it was represented to him that attacks with inadequate forces on so powerful an enemy could only lead to his own destruction, he replied that he could not die in a better cause.

The Companies were then overrunning France. Young Jayme enlisted Englishmen, Frenchmen, and Provençals, the funds being supplied by his Queen. He advanced with his little army to Narbonne, and thence to Toulouse. His beloved sister Isabel, who had become the wife of the Marquis of Monserrat, joined her brother when he invaded his own territory of Roussillon. The town of Perpignan was too strong for attack, and the Ceremonious one was making great preparations for the defence of Catalonia. His army was assembled in the Ampurdan to oppose an entry by the Pass of Panizas. The young King of Majorca therefore crossed the Pyrenees, entering by the Puig-cerdan Pass, and occupied the county of Urgel. His uncle of Aragon resorted to a way more in accordance with his nature than a fair fight. He poisoned his nephew. The secret crime was perpetrated at Valderan, near Urgel. Jayme died in his sister's arms, rendering up a life which had been devoted to the memory of his unhappy father. It was in January 1375 that the last King of Majorca and King Consort of Naples expired within his own rightful dominions of Cerdaña. His body was buried in the Franciscan monastery of Soria. His sister Isabel returned into Gascony, and died in 1379, the last of her race.

Pedro IV., the Ceremonious, after a turbulent reign of fifty years, occupied chiefly in unjust quarrels with his relations and neighbours, at last died in 1396. His sons, Martin and Juan, were rightful heirs to Majorca, the family of their Majorcan cousins having become extinct. His daughter Leonor, wife of Juan I. of Castille, was the mother of Henry III. of Castille, and also of Fernando (surnamed of Antequera from having taken that town from the Moors), who, when the male line of Aragon failed on the death of King Martin, became King of Aragon.

An ancient and most touching memorial of Jayme IV. and his sister Isabel is still preserved at Alfavia by the descendants of their true and faithful friends of the Santa Cilia family. The estate was held by the Santa Cilia family for five generations, when the heiress Leonor married Gabriel de Berga. The heiress of Berga married Zaforteza, and Don Josè Burguez Zaforteza is now the owner of Alfavia and guardian of the relic.

The country seat of Alfavia, at the foot of the mountain pass leading to the valley of Soller, is surrounded by enchanting scenery. In front there are two fir-clad mountain-peaks, with just a peep between them of the garden of Palma, the cathedral, and the blue Mediterranean. All round there are precipitous mountains, the lower slopes in terraces planted with lemon and orange trees. The beautiful garden is famous for a long pergola covered with flowing creepers, having a fountain in each arch on either side. The entrance to the courtyard is by a wide and lofty passage, and the first compartment of its roof is a reminder of the Moorish origin of the house. It is a dome in the style of the roofs at the Alhambra, the colours still visible. Round the margin, or cornice, there is an Arabic inscription, which has been thus translated:

'Precept is of God: power is of God: mercy is of God: God is most great, there is no God but Him: wealth consists in God.'

On the walls of the passage the coats-of-arms are painted of the families which have owned Alfavia since Moorish times:

  I. Ben nassar (*or a lion rampant gules*).

 II. Santa Cilia (*argent three bars gules*).

III. Berga (*azure five crescents or*).

IV. Burgues (*or twelve crescents azure*).

 V. Zaforteza (*gules three fleurs-de-lys or*).

But the great treasure of Alfavia is the memorial of the unfortunate brother and sister, Jayme IV. and Isabel. It consists of a solid oaken armchair of the fourteenth century, designed and carved for Arnaldo de Santa Cilia in loving memory of his ill-fated friends. The workmanship and the costumes of the figures carved on it are the evidence of its date. The carvings represent the sorrows of the two unfortunate children of Jayme III. On each end of the back there are lions séjant. On the back, facing the seat, two figures are carved, a prince and a lady, in costumes of the fourteenth century. They are seated at a table, supposed to be a chessboard, but the surface is smooth. A small dog is under the table. Over them there is a tree with three branches, and foliage at the end of each. On each branch, among the foliage, there is a bird of evil omen or of mourning—crows and owl—

symbolising the sorrows of the two young people beneath them. Below the seat there are two fierce bloodhounds facing each other, one killing a rabbit.

At the back of the chair the carving is still more symbolical. A laurel-tree rises out of a tomb, and among its foliage there is a crowned head, intended for that of Jayme III. On either side of the tree stand the same prince and princess, the prince with a hawk on his wrist. Both point their hands down to the tomb, in which there is the same crowned head.

In a lower compartment there is a fierce hound chasing a rabbit; and beneath that again there is a rabbit sitting up and looking back behind a mound, a second mound with a rabbit looking out of it, and the hindquarters of another going into its hole. On the sides of the chair there are niches with arches, and under two of them on either side are armed figures in iron caps, shirts of mail, swords, and shields. One is crowned and has a long mantle, and a bird with wings displayed is carved on his shield.[18]

The whole composition is very curious and most interesting, alike a touching memorial of the brother and sister, the last of their race, and a very precious relic of antiquity.

The descendants of the second son of Jayme the Conqueror have left a goodly record. To them Majorca owed her rights and liberties, the settlement of her people, the founding of her towns, and all the beginnings of her future prosperity. Devoted to the good of their people, honourable and true to their word, wise in counsel, steadfast in adversity, they produced also knights-errant of the most chivalrous type, like En Fernando and like young Jayme IV., the last of his race.

CHAPTER XIII
RELATES THE STORY, SO FAR AS IT CONCERNS MAJORCA, OF THE LAST KINGS OF ARAGON

The extinction of their reigning dynasty was a great calamity to the people of Majorca, especially during the prolonged life of the Ceremonious one. At last he died in 1387. His sons were very different in all respects. Juan I., surnamed the Huntsman, succeeded as King of Aragon, and he was also the legitimate heir to the Balearic Islands. A pestilence in Catalonia led him to visit Majorca. He and his Queen were in different galleys, and were separated during bad weather. Juan landed at Soller on July 16, 1394, and proceeded to the castle of Valdemosa. The Queen, reached Palma safely. They were united at the castle of Belver, where they spent six pleasant months. Devoted to the chase, Juan went about over the island hawking the partridges introduced by King Sancho. He also imported deer. Returning to Aragon, he was unfortunately killed in the forest of Foxà, near his castle of Uriols, when hunting a she-wolf. He only had a daughter named Violante, who became Queen of Naples, mother of Louis, Duke of Calabria.

Juan I. was succeeded by his brother King Martin, an excellent prince, surnamed 'the Humane.' At this time San Vicente Ferrer of Valencia was flourishing and striving to create a religious revival, and his zeal made an impression on the minds of King Martin and many of his subjects. In 1413 San Vicente went to Majorca, where his preaching aroused the people to make great demonstrations of their religious fervour. It is even said that the saint wrought a miracle by bringing down abundant rain during a season of drought. The Catholic zeal of King Martin led him to grant Sancho's castle of Valdemosa to the Carthusians for a monastery on June 15, 1399. Large donations for the building of the church were received from Majorcan nobles, and the courtly apartments of King Sancho were converted into cells, a refectory, and a cloister. The Cartuja of Valdemosa continued to flourish on this beautiful site for more than four centuries. The church is a fine edifice, containing the richly carved stalls of the Carthusians, a profile in relief of King Martin, and a remarkably good statue, carved in wood, of St. Bruno. After the suppression and the expulsion of the Carthusians in 1834 their cells were let to families from Palma and others for the summer. A large portion forms the summer residence of Don Juan Sureda, who has converted the refectory into a charming ballroom, with a stage and proscenium at one end for private theatricals. Georges Sand, with the composer Chopin, occupied two of the cells. Georges Sand afterwards wrote a book on her winter residence in Majorca in 1835, animadverting on the country and the people. But her strictures are unfair and, to a great extent, untrue, and have been ably refuted by a native author. To this day the Cartuja on its ridge, surrounded by orange-groves, is a beautiful object in the ascent from the garden of Palma to Valdemosa, still looking more like the castle of King Sancho than a Cartuja. Apartments are shown as having been the residence of King Martin, but he never visited the island personally.

Martin died in 1410 without legitimate children, and there were several claimants to the succession. The Count of Urgel represented the male line, as the grandson of Jayme, brother of Pedro IV. Fernando of Antequera, brother of the King of Castille, was a nephew of King Martin through his mother, Leonor. Louis of Calabria was a grandson of Juan I. and grand-nephew of King Martin. Alfonso, Duke of Gandia, was a nephew of Alfonso IV. and first cousin of Pedro IV. There was also Fadrique, Count of Luna, an illegitimate son of King Martin. Altogether five claimants. Elected delegates from Aragon, Catalonia, Valencia, and Majorca were assembled to examine the claims. There was a strong feeling in favour of the Count of Urgel, as representing the male line; but Fernando de Antequera was chosen, it is supposed through the influence of San Vicente Ferrer. Fernando I. only reigned for four years, from 1412 to 1416, and was succeeded by his son Alfonso V., who devoted a long reign of forty-two years chiefly to the conquest of Naples. He was surnamed 'the Magnanimous.'

The Majorcans gave King Alfonso assistance in soldiers and in ships, and many of their knights served in the King's campaigns. Both the Government and private persons co-operated with Barcelona in fitting out armed ships for the protection of trade against the Barbary pirates. Among the Majorcan nobles who equipped such vessels the foremost was En Salvador Sureda, who also appeared at this time as a knight of chivalry under the following circumstances.

A Catalan knight named Francisco de Valseca, who was famous for his prowess in all jousting exercises, came to Palma to take part in a tournament in 1442. He ran a lance with Salvador Sureda, and censured his opponent for the way in which he had gained an advantage. Sureda replied that he had used his lance and run the course as became a knight, and that he was ready to encounter his adversary again as often as he liked and at any place he might appoint. Valseca did not hear these words because his vizor was down, and he was not told of them until after his return to Barcelona. He then promptly sent a trumpet to Sureda, challenging him to a combat. The two knights sent a joint request to the King, Alfonso V. of Aragon, that he would appoint lists and preside at the encounter. The King consented, naming his city of Naples as the place and summoning the combatants to appear there on a certain day. The royal missive was sent to Sureda, who, on August 23, 1443, sent his trumpet, named Agustin de Luna, with two letters—one of thanks to the King; the other, with a copy of the royal letter, to Valseca. The trumpet sailed from Porto Pi and duly delivered the letters. The day appointed was January 5, 1444.

Both knights proceeded to Naples and made their appearance on the appointed day. En Salvador Sureda wore a crimson surcoat embroidered with gold, and his horse was similarly caparisoned. His device was a small falcon's cage, with the motto 'dentro está quier le cage.' He was preceded by three knights richly dressed, and three pages with the helmet and plumes. The route along which he came was kept by several friends, bearing the well-known Majorcan names of Dameto, Zaforteza, Bosch, Mari, and Vivot. In advance of all was a herald, with trumpets and minstrels and the Sureda standard, which was a cork-tree on a golden ground. Valseca also came splendidly accoutred and similarly attended.

At each end of the lists there were tents for the combatants, and on the side a very richly ornamented pavilion for King Alfonso and his young son Fernando, of whom the King was very fond. Ten knights, called the 'ten faithful ones,' guarded the lists, and two others, nominated by the King, were named 'preservers of peace.' At least twenty thousand spectators were present.

There was complete silence, until a clarion sounded and the two knights came out of their tents and mounted. On a second blast of the clarion the two knights put their lances in rest and commenced their furious careers. At that moment the King threw his warder down, as our poor Richard II. had done some fifty years before, but with very different consequences. The 'ten faithful ones' then rushed between the combatants and wrested their lances from them. Their astonishment was mingled with anger not immediately appeased. Young Fernando then came down from the pavilion and called the two knights, who had dismounted. He told them that the King his father was unwilling that either knight should be killed, both being so distinguished and both having sufficiently proved their fortitude, resolution, and valour. Valseca and Sureda both placed themselves under the orders of the King. The young Prince took a position himself between the two, and, taking a hand of each, he led them up to King Alfonso, at whose feet they knelt and did homage. The King obliged them to make friends, conferred several benefits on them, and the day ended in rejoicing and festivities. The standard of Sureda was hung in the cathedral of Palma. There it remained until 1819, when it was burnt at the fire of the ancient chapel of San Pedro.

Alfonso V. had achieved the conquest of Naples, though he lost his brother Pedro during the siege. When he died, in 1458, his illegitimate son

Fernando succeeded as King of Naples, followed by his sons Alfonso and Federigo. On their deaths Naples became part of the vast dominions of Fernando of Aragon and Castille. Thus Alfonso V. restored all the dominions of King Manfred to his descendants.

The conqueror of Naples was succeeded as King of Aragon by his brother Juan II., a very different man. Juan had married Blanche, the heiress of Navarre, by whom he had a son Carlos, Prince of Viana, and a daughter Leonor. Juan II. began to persecute his son in 1450, before his accession, and when he was only King of Navarre by right of his wife. Carlos, when he came of age, felt that he was the rightful King of Navarre, and not his father. He took up arms, was defeated, and taken prisoner. He was confined in the castle of Monroy, but he escaped to Naples, and after the death of his uncle Alfonso he took refuge in Sicily. Juan II. sent an envoy to induce the Prince of Viana to come to Majorca, where he landed in August 1459, and was very cordially received by the people. Juan II. published an order that all the castles in Majorca were to be delivered over to the Prince; but he sent a secret order at the same time that some of the strongest, including the castle of Belver, were not to be given up, and that Carlos was to be detained if he entered Belver. Knowing that the word of his father could not be depended upon, and fearful of arrest, the Prince resolved to proceed to Barcelona and seek an interview. He landed on March 20, 1460, and his father pretended to be reconciled, fearing insurrections in his son's favour; but the Prince of Viana died, under very suspicious circumstances, in the following year. His sister Leonor then became Queen of Navarre, and by her marriage with Gaston de Foix the title descended to Henry IV., and again became merged in the crown of France.

Juan II. had married secondly Juana Henriquez, daughter of the Admiral of Castille, and by her he had a son Fernando, and a daughter Juana, Queen of Naples. After a reign of twenty years Juan II. died, and was succeeded by his son Fernando II. in 1479. The marriage of Fernando with Isabella of Castille united the two kingdoms, and Majorca, with the other islands, became a part of the kingdom of Spain. But Majorca retained her constitution and privileges during the sway of the Austrian dynasty.

CHAPTER XIV
THE MAJORCANS AS NAVIGATORS

The intelligence and energy of the Catalans of Barcelona and Majorca, combined with their industry and perseverance, raised the kingdom of Aragon to a very important position as a maritime Power in the Mediterranean. Long the rivals of the Genoese, the Catalans at one time gained complete ascendency. Their fleets dominated the western half of the great inland sea, with Sicily, Sardinia, Corsica, Malta, and the Balearic Islands either under the sovereignty or in close alliance with the Kings of Aragon. Their trading vessels frequented the Levant and the Ægean Sea, and Catalan consulates and factories were established in Macedonia, in Greece, and on the islands. Voyages were even undertaken beyond the Pillars of Hercules.

The seamen of Majorca were as energetic and expert as those of the mainland, and Palma had a great dockyard and arsenal where galleys of thirty benches were built. But the success of the Catalans depended more on their skill and superior knowledge of navigation than on the size and number of their ships. In the middle of the fourteenth century the marine service of Majorca consisted of 30,600 sailors, manning 460 vessels, of which twenty-four were of the largest size, and the others were used for carrying merchandise.[19] Palma could fit out a contingent of large ships as part of the armed fleet of Aragon, and the safety of trade was provided for both by the Government and by private enterprise. Salvador de Sureda was not the only Majorcan notable who fitted out a ship at his own expense to resist the incursions of Barbary pirates.

The natives of Majorca were for a long time the leading geographers, inventors of instruments, and constructors of marine charts in Europe. They used the magnetic needle long before its supposed discovery by Gioia of Amalfi, and they could find the polar distance. The rudeness of their instruments increases the merit of the results obtained with them. Their *portolani*, or marine charts, were far more accurate than any of the maps even of a later period. They were in constant use before 1359, when every galley was ordered to carry two charts for navigation.[20] Several Catalan *portolani* have been preserved. The most interesting, though not the oldest, is now in the possession of the Count of Montenegro at Palma. It was drawn in 1439 by Gabriel de Valseca, who in his own hand wrote the following inscription on it: 'gabriell de ualsequa la feta en Malorcha an MCCCCXXXVIIII.' It once belonged to Amerigo Vespucci, as an inscription on the back testifies: 'questa ampia pelle di geografia fue pagata de Amerigo Vespucio CXX ducati di oro di marco.' It was bought at

Florence in the eighteenth century by Cardinal Despuig, to form part of the library of his nephew, the Count of Montenegro. A facsimile was made for the Spanish Government at the time of the Columbus anniversary, and now hangs in the museum of the Ministry of Marine at Madrid.

A curious accident happened to this priceless geographical document in 1839. Georges Sand obtained leave to see it. Up to that time the stiff parchment had been rolled up in a tin case. It was brought out and spread on a table. The famous novelist, to keep it down, took up an inkstand and placed it on the edge of the map. But the parchment, which had been rolled up for centuries, was too strong. It flew back and the ink was upset. Georges Sand, horrified at what she had done, ran straight out of the house. Luckily the injury was not serious, and is confined to the part outside the Mediterranean. The precious map now has a room to itself in the Montenegro palace at Palma. It is framed and glazed on both sides, and kept in a locked case covered with crimson velvet.

The outline of the Mediterranean is almost exactly correct. The lines of the Valseca *portolano* placed over the coast-lines of a modern chart correspond very nearly, especially the western part. Italy is slightly out in longitude. The Valseca *portolano* includes Great Britain, Ireland, Jutland, the Euxine and Persian Gulf, and the Red Sea painted bright red. The chart is covered with rhumb-lines. The Nile is separated into two, one taken through Abyssinia and the other away to the Niger region. There are kings on their thrones, and every country has its arms painted on flags. The golden shield of Aragon, with its four pales gules, flies over Aragon, Majorca, Sardinia, and Sicily. It is interesting to see the south of Spain painted green, for the Moors were still at Granada. There are several legends in minute handwriting on the map. Majorca may well be proud of having in her island in this priceless map the most valuable and interesting geographical document of the fifteenth century. Next to it comes the *mapa mondi* of Jayme Cresques, also of Catalonian origin, and now in the Bibliothèque Nationale of Paris.

The fame of the geographers of Majorca, for their profound knowledge as navigators and skill as cartographers, spread over Europe. When Prince Henry founded his celebrated school for pilots at Sagres, as an essential part of his plans for the discovery of the African coast, he found no one more competent to direct it than 'Maestro Jacome de Mallorca,' a most able navigator and constructor of nautical instruments. But the Majorcan sailors did not confine themselves to these important studies, nor to cruises in the Mediterranean. They undertook voyages beyond the Pillars of Hercules in very early times. On August 10, 1346, Jayme Ferrar set sail from Palma, passed through the Straits, and coasted along Africa as far as the mouth of the Rio del Oro, five degrees south of that Cape Nun which the Portuguese did not round until 1419.

The commercial prosperity of Majorca, derived from the enterprise of her sailors, led to the building of the *Lonja*, or Exchange, which is still one of the chief architectural ornaments of Palma. The architect was Guillem Sagrera, who also built the Castel Nuovo at Naples for Alfonso V.; and the work was undertaken by the principal merchants of Palma. Finished in 1450, it consists of a lofty hall with a groined roof supported by six tall slender pillars. The doorway is very richly carved in the style of the north door of the cathedral, and at each angle of the edifice there is a statue of a saint under a stone canopy: San Nicolas in the angle facing Porto Pi, in the opposite niche San Juan Bautista, in the angle looking towards the Ataranza (arsenal) Santa Catalina, and Santa Clara looking towards the Almudaina.[21] Here was the centre of commercial transactions during the Middle Ages, while the wharves outside formed an active and busy scene, the ceaseless ebb and flow of Mediterranean trade. The commercial ventures were not without danger, the piratical States of Barbary continuing their raids and depredations quite into modern times.

Barbarossa infested the seas and caused such havoc that the Emperor Charles V. undertook punitive expeditions to Tunis in 1535 and to Algiers in 1541. On the latter occasion he landed at Alcudia, and proceeded thence to Palma on October 13. He was received with great demonstrations of joy by all the chief people of the island, Nicolas Cotoner and Pedro Juan de Santa Cilia, bearers of most ancient names, walking by his horse to the cathedral, where Mass was said. The Emperor was received in the Almudaina, and Leonardo Zaforteza superintended the arrangements for lodging the other guests. Charles departed on the 18th, taking with him a hundred Majorcan knights who joined his expedition. But the elements were against them, and the invasion of Algiers ended in failure.

The Moors were not slow to retaliate. Two years afterwards five hundred of them landed at Pollenza, but were repulsed with heavy loss. Several other descents were made on the island by Dragut and his subordinate corsairs, and there was much hard fighting, with slaughter on both sides, but serious loss of unfortunate people carried off into slavery. It was in September 1552 that Valdemosa was attacked by the crews of the Algerine galleots. About five hundred Moors landed in the night and entered the town without opposition. Loading themselves with spoils and taking four hundred captives with them, they began their retreat to the ships. Raimondo Gual had command of only thirty-five men at Valdemosa. Open resistance would have been futile; still, he watched his opportunity. In a narrow pass, since called 'Pàs dels Mòros,' he made a sudden attack on the retreating pirates, who were panic-stricken, and very few escaped. No quarter was given to them. Their banner was hung up in the parish church. Valdemosa was again unsuccessfully attacked by the Moors in 1582.

Next it was the turn of the town of Andraix, at the south-west end of the island, which was attacked by twenty-four piratical vessels in 1553. The inhabitants fled, some taking refuge in a small castle. Don Jorge Fortuñy, a neighbouring proprietor, put himself at the head of a small body of cavalry, and his name alone led the invaders to make a hasty retreat to their ships. But Andraix was attacked and pillaged in 1555, and again in 1578.

In 1561 a piratical expedition was fitted out at Algiers, consisting of twenty-two vessels, under the command of a renegade named Ochali, to attack the town of Soller. Measures were taken for its defence, and troops arrived under a commander named Miguel Angelats. Fearing the fortress at the port of Soller, the pirates landed at a place called 'Coll de la Illa' 1,700 men in two divisions. One division marched to the port, while the other advanced by the bridge of *Binibaci* to attack the town. Angelats had left the town, leading his troops to oppose the landing, but was too late. Thus the Moors entered and pillaged Soller without opposition. But the Majorcans returned with all speed and, in a desperate fight, completely routed the pirates, who lost at least five hundred of their number. Don Guillem de Rocafull, the Viceroy of Majorca, hurried across the island with succour, and found that the victory was already won.

There were other piratical raids on the island, showing the great need for vigilance and for a protecting fleet. But the maritime power was not so strong or efficient in the sixteenth century as it had been in the more flourishing times when the Aragonese kings reigned and so successfully promoted the maritime eminence of their subjects. Nevertheless, the sailors of Majorca continued to maintain the fair fame of their ancestors, and have done so to the present day.

CHAPTER XV
THE COMUNIDADES

The rising of the people of Spain against their rulers coincided in point of time with the accession of the Austrian dynasty in the person of Charles V. In the Castilles it was a very noble attempt of the towns, under the leadership of patriots such as Padilla, to preserve the constitutional liberties of the people. It failed, but the best feeling of the country will always look back to it with approval and with pride. The picture of the execution of Padilla now has an honoured place in the hall of the Cortes at Madrid, and the story of the Comunidades of Castille has occupied the pen of one of Spain's most accomplished historians.
But in the risings of so-called Comuneros in Valencia and in Majorca there is no such noble story to tell. These were mere insurrections of artisans and peasantry, goaded on by the violent harangues of leaders as ignorant as themselves, without fixed aims or objects, and influenced only by envy and jealousy of those who were placed above them. From Valencia the contagion spread to Majorca in 1521. The people, called *pageses*, and inhabitants of the country towns, complained that the nobles, living in their palaces at Palma, oppressed them with taxes and misgoverned the country. The insurrection began with a meeting of artisans in a house near the church of San Nicolas in Palma, where an inflammatory speech was addressed to them by a man named Juan Crespi. The movement rapidly spread, and came to the notice of the Viceroy, Don Miguel de Gurrea. He called a meeting of officials, but the only result was the arrest of a shoemaker named Pedro Begur and three others. The Viceroy had no sufficient force at his command, and the arrests only infuriated the mob, who flew to arms and liberated the prisoners. The Viceroy then rode through the streets with some attendants, calling on the rioters to disperse, and promising to listen to their complaints. The insurgents then occupied the public buildings, seized all the arms they could find, and chose Juan Crespi to be their captain. This was in the end of January 1521. Crespi's title was 'Instador del beneficio comun'; and the Viceroy, to gain time, actually issued a decree conferring it upon him. In February both the Viceroy and the insurgents sent letters to the King, giving different versions of what had taken place. In March the insurgents had organised a force of 1,800 men and had got possession of all the gates of the city. Many of the nobles were killed, and the rest escaped to Alcudia, a fortified town. The Viceroy escaped to the island of Iviça.
The Jurados, consisting of Juan de Puigdorfila, Jayme Marti, and two others, were allowed to remain in office nominally; but fifteen

'Conservadores' were elected by the insurgents to introduce the reforms they demanded. In April a reply came from the King to the 'Instador' and the 'Conservadores,' ordering them to obey the Viceroy, who would do them justice. They declared the letter to be a forgery, and proceeded to acts of violence, beheading all who openly opposed them. The movement spread to the country towns, and the loyal people were in a state of terror. Some of the nobles had taken refuge in the castle of Belver, under the protection of Pedro Pax, the castellan. On July 29 the insurgents began the siege of the castle, which was gallantly defended until all the ammunition was expended. The place was then taken by assault. The insurgents beheaded the castellan and several others. The castle was gutted and left in charge of three men to guard it.

There is a long list of nobles who were put to death at Palma, including a Cotoner, five Puigdorfilas, and a Despuig. Pedro Juan Zaforteza took refuge in Valdemosa, whence he escaped, in the disguise of a friar, to Alcudia, where the rest of the nobles had taken refuge. In November 1521 the insurgents formed an army of six thousand men, including cavalry, and six siege pieces, to lay siege to Alcudia. The town was surrounded on November 20, 1521, the besiegers being busy constructing scaling ladders and a battery for their artillery. The nobles made a very resolute sally, capturing the battery with its guns and stores, which disheartened the besiegers, upwards of a hundred being killed. Antonio Sureda especially distinguished himself in this sally, and the hopes of the besieged rose high. Pedro Pax, son of the castellan of Belver, was chosen to command at Alcudia. He found that provisions were running short, and resolved to attack the enemy with his whole force, numbering 1,080. The battle was long contested, but at last the insurgents broke and fled, thus raising the siege. Their provisions and stores were captured, and the scaling ladders and other siege appliances were burnt.

In August Charles V. sent Dr. Francisco Ubaque as Regent to restore order, the Viceroy being still in the island of Iviça. He landed at Alcudia. The insurgents were then in occupation of the neighbouring town of Puebla. They resumed the siege of Alcudia in September, but they were again repulsed after a very desperate attempt to carry the place by assault.

The Emperor was at Brussels, and at last he was induced to attend to the deplorable condition of Majorca. An expedition was ordered to be fitted out in the Catalonian ports to restore order and punish the delinquents. Four large galleys, thirteen ships, and several smaller vessels were fitted out, and 1,200 men were embarked under the command of Don Francisco Carroz and Don Juan Velasco. The expedition first went to Iviça to embark the Viceroy, Don Miguel de Gurrea or Urrea.

On October 15 the fleet entered the port of Pollenza. The rescuers were received with great joy at Alcudia, where the Viceroy proclaimed a general pardon to those who laid down their arms and returned to obedience. Many came in, surrendering under the terms of the proclamation; but others held out. At Palma there was great confusion, the Bishop, Dr. Pont, working incessantly to induce the people to submit.

At Pollenza the insurgents made a desperate resistance and there was great slaughter, no quarter being given. Very few escaped to the mountains. On November 5 the Viceroy, with all the chief officers and three thousand soldiers, left Alcudia and advanced to Puebla, where they only found two labourers and a priest. Other towns were found without inhabitants. At Inca the people came out with their priests to meet the Viceroy, singing a *Te Deum*. On March 1, 1523, the Viceroy invested Palma with his army. Priamo de Villalonga had held out in the castle of the Templars, then called the Royal Castle, for many months. He was now relieved, and this disastrous insurrection approached its end.

The last act of this melancholy drama was performed and described by young Don Alonzo Enriquez de Guzman in his very entertaining autobiography. He was ordered by the Viceroy of Valencia to take command of five hundred men, and to sail from Murviedro, to reinforce the army that was employed in re-establishing order in Majorca. But the five hundred men refused to embark until they had received their arrears of pay. After a great deal of trouble he at length persuaded them to go on board, and they sailed to join the army in Majorca in nine small vessels. Arriving off Palma at nightfall, Don Alonzo, a young man in his twenty-third year, but with an amount of self-assurance beyond his age, announced the arrival of a very important reinforcement. The report was spread that his force consisted of five thousand men. Captain Crispin, the leader of the rebels, came out of the town with a guard of fifty men and sought speech with Don Alonzo. He besought the young commander to mediate between him and the Viceroy and induce him to consent to a deputation being sent to the Emperor. He proposed that, while the deputies were going and coming, Don Alonzo should remain in the city with thirty men, Crispin promising to deliver the place to whomsoever the King should command.

Don Alonzo, with the approval of the Viceroy, agreed to this and entered the city, the Viceroy's army being encamped outside. After a month the deputies returned, reporting that the Emperor had listened to them every day for two hours during eight days, and that they were very well satisfied. Nine days afterwards an order came to Don Alonzo from the Emperor, and another from the Viceroy, which were delivered to him through the closed gates. The Emperor instructed him to obey the Viceroy. The order of the Viceroy was that he should seize the person of Crispin and those of the thirteen members of his Council, and open the gates at four o'clock that afternoon, being March 7, 1522. If the people would not let him do so, he was to come out himself.

The orders came to Don Alonzo at ten in the forenoon. He at once proceeded to the Plaza de Cort, where he found Crispin with his guards and five of his councillors. He told them that he had received orders to deliver up the city to Don Miguel de Urrea, the Viceroy, and expressed a hope that they would keep faith and give evidence to the Emperor that they were honest men. Crispin replied that he would be the first to obey the orders of his Majesty. The rest all said the same.

Don Alonzo then went to dinner in the Almudaina, and each man departed to his own house. After dinner he called an assembly, ordering no one to bring his arms. Then, with many kind words, he put Crispin and all his councillors in irons. This manœuvre having been safely accomplished, he formed processions, with all the women and children barefooted on one side and all the men barefooted on the other, and made them go to the gates and open them, with loud cries for mercy. The Viceroy and Don Juan de Velasco entered at the head of their troops, Don Alonzo meeting them with the keys of the city, and saying: 'The gates are now open, and the desires of the people are turned to serve the King and your Lordship. They seek for pardon.'

The Viceroy did not answer. He entered the city and executed what he called justice. Crispin was cut into four quarters, as were all his thirteen councillors. The number of persons who were hanged and quartered was 420.Such is the account of the surrender of Palma given by an eyewitness and actor in the sanguinary drama.[22] One side seems to have been every bit as bloodthirsty as the other. Time alone could heal the wounds. Don Alonzo was sent to Iviça with his five hundred men, where he did good service against Barbarossa and his pirates.From the first rising to the restoration of order, the troubles had lasted for more than two years.Don Miguel de Gurrea or Urrea, the Viceroy, who had shown so much prudence at the commencement when he was powerless, and so much courage as soon as he had troops at his disposal, sent the keys of the kingdom to the Emperor. Keys finely worked in gold were sent in their place, which the descendants of Gurrea preserve to this day. Alcudia received the title of 'the most faithful city.'The principal nobles who valorously resisted the rebellion and restored order were Priamo de Villalonga, Alfonso Torrella, Salvador Sureda, Jayme Oleza, Matias Fortuñy, Mateo Togores, Albertin Damato, Antonio Gual, Zaforteza, Despuig, Cotoner—all names which appear in the annals of their country, from generation to generation, down to this day.The insurrection caused great misery and destruction of property, and it was quite a century before the islanders can be said to have recovered from its evil effects, either morally or as regards their industries and general well-being.

CHAPTER XVI
THE MAJORCAN HISTORIANS—WAR OF SUCCESSION—FAMILIES ENNOBLED—COTONERS—RAXA AND CARDINAL DESPUIG—COUNTRY HOUSES

With the war of the 'Comunidades' the romance of Majorcan history ends. During the seventeenth century the country was very slowly recovering from the effects of that disastrous rising; but it was long before the good relations between the different classes of the people were restored. The island was governed under the Kings of the House of Austria by Viceroys, of whom five were natives of Majorca. The names of Moncada, Fuster, Pax, Zaforteza, and Sureda occur in the list.

But though the making of history seemed to be dead, the work of recording the glorious annals of Majorca under her own kings was zealously undertaken by natives of the island. The first official chronicler, appointed by the Jurados, was Don Juan Dameto. He wrote the 'Historia General del reino Balearico' between 1621 and 1631, and died prematurely in 1633. His work commences with the earliest Roman times and is brought down to the death of Jayme II. Dameto had travelled much and was an accomplished scholar. His work is by no means a mere chronicle. The style is agreeable and full without being prolix, and shows a sense of proportion and of the relative importance of events.

Don Vicente Mut, who was born at Palma in 1614, was the continuator of Dameto. He was a military man and major of the militia of his island, an accomplished mathematician, as well as a student of history. He searched the archives with great diligence, and gives valuable details respecting the administration of the island at different periods. His history covers the ground from the accession of King Sancho to the suppression of the 'Comunidades,' and contains spirited accounts of the raids of Barbary pirates and histories of the monasteries and hospitals. Mut died in 1687.

With him our accessible island histories end, for the history of Geronimo Alemany, which would bring the record down to the death of Charles II., the last King of the House of Austria, is still in manuscript. We have to thank Don Miguel Moragues Pro and Don Joaquim Maria Bover for having edited the histories of Dameto and Mut, with very copious notes. The three thick volumes were published at Palma in 1841, and a fourth volume containing the history by Alemany was promised. Visitors to Palma who take an intelligent interest in the history of the island will desire to possess and to read them. They will find the three volumes at the excellent book-seller's shop of Don Felipe Guasp, No. 6 Morey Street, the first turn to the right after crossing the Plaza de Santa Eulalia.

The eighteenth century opened with the war of succession. The French claimant was a grandson of a sister of Charles II. The German claimant was a grandson of Charles's aunt. Catalonia and Majorca espoused the cause of the German archduke, while the rest of Spain proclaimed the French prince as Philip V. On October 1, 1706, Majorca was occupied by the troops of the Archduke Charles, and all adherents of the French claimant were persecuted or banished. Even after the fall of Barcelona the Majorcans held out. But all was in vain. In June 1715 a large army landed and besieged Palma, which capitulated after a siege of seventeen days, and the Bourbons forced the islanders to submit to their yoke. All the ancient privileges and grants of the Aragonese monarchs to the Majorcans were abolished, with their form of government. Captains-general were substituted for the Viceroys, and the present fortifications of Palma were constructed in the reign of Philip V. Majorca suffered from the misgovernment of Bourbon rule with the rest of Spain. From that time the people have had to rely upon their own virility, energy, and skill for any advance in civilisation and well-being, and not in vain. The Majorcans steadily progressed, while their old families, claiming descent from the soldiers of King Jayme, became distinguished in arms and letters and were ennobled, several as early as the times of the Austrian kings. In 1625 the title of Marquis of Bellpuig was given to the family of Dameto y Cotoner, in 1632 that of Santa Maria de Formiguera to the family of Burgues Zaforteza y Villalonga, in 1634 that of Count of Ayamans to the family of Togores (formerly Moncada), in 1658 that of Count of Montenegro to the family of Despuig, and in 1717 that of Count of Ariañy to the family of Cotoner. Several titles were also conferred on Majorcan families during the eighteenth century; generally well deserved.[23]

Among the distinguished sons of the Cotoner family was Rafael Cotoner, who was Grand Master of Malta from 1660 to 1663. He built Fort Ricasoli and the lines which are still known as the Cotonera. His brother, Nicolas Cotoner, was Grand Master from 1663 to 1680. An almost equally distinguished member of this family was the late General Cotoner, who was Governor of Porto Rico, and was devotedly attached to his native island and her interests.

But it was to members of the ancient family of Despuig that Majorca owed its fame as a place of cultured learning during the eighteenth century. Descended from Bernardo Despuig, a companion of the Conqueror Jayme I., the family has always been closely connected with the history of the island. Among them Juan Bautista Despuig served at Lepanto and in Flanders; but his best title to fame was that he devoted his wealth to the promotion of the well-being of his poorer neighbours and won the title of

'Father of the Poor.' His grandson did such good service as a military commander that in 1658 he was created Count of Montenegro. The first Count's son, Bernardo, was Grand Master of the Order of St. John of Jerusalem at Malta from 1736 to 1741. Juan Despuig, the second Count of Montenegro and also Count of Montoro by right of his mother, espoused the Bourbon side in the War of Succession, and suffered a long imprisonment in the castle of Belver from 1706 to 1715, the period of the Austrian occupation of the island. Many other members of the family were distinguished for their services to the State. The best-known is Dr. Don Antonio Despuig, who was Archbishop of Valencia and of Seville and Cardinal of San Calisto, a prelate not more famed for his learning than for the love he always showed for his island home.

Cardinal Despuig has left many memorials which will ever secure for him an honourable place in the island's history. He devoted both time, money, and a cultivated taste to enriching the country seat of his nephew, the Count of Montenegro, as well as his palace in Palma, with the most precious literary and artistic productions of Italy and Spain.

The country seat of Raxa is a place of enchantment at the foot of the mountains, approached from Palma through miles of almond-groves in full blossom during February. In Moorish times it was called Araxa, and was granted by King Jayme I. to the Count of Ampurias, becoming the property of the family of Despuig in 1620. Raxa is a large house of three storeys, built round a courtyard, with an ancient elm-tree in the centre. The rooms are exceedingly numerous, and all the furniture is of a date at least 150 years ago. There are many beautiful Florentine cabinets, some good pictures, and fayence. The dining-room has a carved oak ceiling in squares, with an old fayence plate let into each. One room is full of valuable Vatican engravings, another of paintings of Rome as it was 150 years ago. One side of the house has balconies, with arcades, looking on the garden and over a lovely view. The great glory of Raxa is the museum of Roman sculpture. Cardinal Despuig acquired a site near Albano, where once had stood the superb temple to Egeria, built by the Emperor Domitian. Between 1787 and 1796 the Cardinal conducted excavations which brought to light many statues, busts, altars, and other remains, which he sent to Majorca to adorn his nephew's country seat. There is a very fine statue of Trajan, others of Caligula, Hercules, a gladiator, &c. A full descriptive list is given in Bover's 'Noticias Historico-topograficas.'[24] Opposite to the door of the museum is that of the chapel, where there is a picture of Jesus and the Woman of Samaria.

There is a charming garden, with fountains, in front of the house, and orange-groves beyond. Behind there are garden terraces up the mountain side, and two very large tanks. A long flight of steps, with statues on either side and water flowing down in masonry channels, leads up to loftier terraces with flower-beds and groves of cypress, pine-trees, and laurustinus. It is like fairyland; and from a summer-house there are views of the sea of almond-blossoms extending to Palma on one side, and of the pine-clad mountains and serrated peaks on the other.

Many of the treasures collected by the Cardinal are in the Montenegro palace in the city of Palma. This palace, in the street of the same name, has a courtyard with palm-trees, whence a wide stone staircase leads to a gallery, where is the front door. The rooms are large and lofty, richly furnished, and warmed by *braseros*. At the back of the house there is a good-sized garden with palm-trees and an evergreen oak. In this palace are more of the treasures collected by the Cardinal. The famous *portolano* of Valseca has already been fully described. At the top of the house is the magnificent library, arranged in subjects. One of the most valuable books is a manuscript 'Nobiliario' of the Aragonese nobility of the fifteenth century, with coats of arms beautifully painted. Here, too, is the original manuscript of Alemany's history. The poetical and historical works are the most numerous, including fine editions of 'Don Quijote.' The room is of great length, and at the end was the cabinet of coins, Roman Consular and Imperial, Spanish-Arabian, Gothic, and Aragonese kings. According to Bover, the finest collection of Majorcan coins is in the cabinet of the Count of Ayamans.

Cardinal Despuig, who was an intimate friend of Pope Pius VI., died at Lucca on May 2, 1813, leaving to his country a thousand memorials which will give his name an honoured place in the Balearic *fasti*. His nephew, for whom all these collections were made, died in the same year. This Count's son, Ramon, fifth Count of Montenegro, was Captain-General of Majorca, and died in 1848. The present Count, to whose great courtesy our knowledge of Raxa and the Cardinal's treasures is due, is a grandson of the Captain-General, and is the seventh Count of Montenegro.

Majorca boasts other country houses almost as beautiful, though not quite so interesting as Raxa. Alfavia has already been described, and Canet, the home of the Torrellas, has been mentioned. Another charming country seat is La Granja de Esporla, the home of the Fortuñy family. It is in a valley, with mountain-spurs on either side and abundant supplies of water. The house is built round a courtyard, one side having a wide stone passage on the upper storey, with open colonnades. Over the archway into the courtyard there is a stone coat of arms of Fortuñy (*argent five pellets, two, two, and one*; quartering Gual, Despuig, and Zaforteza). There is a very large stone-paved hall, hung with pictures, which opens on to a narrow garden leading to terraces up the mountain-side, fountains, and artificial grottos. In front there is a long pergola of roses, orange and lemon groves, and a splendid old yew-tree.

The mountains are clothed with ilex as well as pine-trees.

There are great advantages in the chief people of the island living in their country houses during the summer and having personal intercourse with their people. It encourages enterprise. Thus at Esporlas there are extensive cloth-factories, and at Canet, under the patronage of the Torrellas, there is a fayence-manufactory, producing vases with very beautiful designs.

CHAPTER XVII
THE MARQUIS OF ROMANA AND THE PATRIOT JOVELLANOS.

The romance of Majorcan history seemed to have come to an end with young Jayme IV. and his sister; but it was renewed in the career of the Marquis of Romana, the most distinguished of later Majorcans.

Like many other noble families of the Peninsula, the Caros derive their coat-armour from an incident in the memorable battle of Las Navas de Tolosa.[25] Juan Caro accompanied En Jayme in the conquest of Majorca. His descendants were in the conquest of Almeria, the wars of Flanders, the battle of Los Gelves, the sea-fight of Lepanto, and many other combats against the enemies of Spain. They held estates in Orihuela, Elche, Crevillente, and Novelda, and the feudal castle of Maza, as well as extensive property in Majorca. Don José Caro was created Marquis of La Romana and Viscount of Benaesa in 1739 for his great services during the War of Succession. Don Pedro Caro, the third Marquis, was born at Palma in 1761, and lost his father, a very distinguished naval officer, when he was only fourteen. The third Marquis entered the navy, rising to the rank of captain of a frigate, but exchanged into the army in order to serve under his uncle, General Ventura Caro, in the first war with revolutionary France. He had risen to the rank of lieutenant-general when Mr. Hookham Frere came to Madrid as Ambassador from England in 1803. They at once became great friends, the Marquis being of immense use to the English diplomatist in explaining to him the state of parties at the Spanish Court. Southey says of Romana that he was 'a man whose happy nature had resisted all the evil and debilitating influences of the age and rank in which he was born. He possessed a rare union of frankness and prudence, while he read with unerring intuition the characters of others. Spain has never produced a man more excellently brave, more dutifully devoted to his country, more free from the taint of selfishness, more truly noble.'

When Napoleon got possession of the resources of Spain and was able to issue his decrees through the corrupt government of Godoy, he sought to weaken those resources in order that Spain might fall an easier prey when the time was ripe. With this object the Marquis of Romana was ordered to march with fourteen thousand men, being the best troops in the Spanish army, to the other end of Europe. This was in August 1807, when Romana's force was quartered at Hamburg and Lubeck. The Spanish contingent was intended to form part of a Franco-Danish army under Bernadotte for the invasion of Sweden. The Spanish regiments were then placed in garrisons at Aarhuus, Ebeltoft, Mariager, Aalborg, and Randers in Jutland, in the island of Funen, and two regiments in Zeeland. They were closely watched and cut off from all intercourse with Spain. But an English squadron under Saumarez effectually prevented an invasion of Sweden.

When the whole of Spain rose against the usurping government of Joseph Bonaparte it became a matter of the utmost importance to communicate the news to Romana and his troops, and to restore them to their country. But it was a service of extreme difficulty. The French cut off all communication and vigilantly intercepted letters; while the Spaniards in Denmark were informed that all their countrymen were unanimous in their allegiance to Joseph. A priest named Robertson, an accomplished linguist, was selected by Mr. Frere to convey the news to Romana. To give him written credentials was too dangerous; but Mr. Frere hit upon a way of convincing Romana that the message was genuine. Robertson was to quote to him a line from the poem of the 'Cid,' with an emendation. When Romana and Frere were at Madrid together, the former advised his English friend to read that poem. One day Romana called upon his friend, when Frere had just made a suggested emendation in the line:

Aun vea el hora que vos *merezca dos* tanto.

Frere suggested *merezcades*, and Romana concurred in its propriety. No one but Romana and Frere knew of this; so that, on quoting it, the Marquis was convinced that Robertson came from Frere. Romana then first heard the real situation of his country. They conversed in Latin. The Spanish general at once resolved to effect his escape from Denmark with his troops, if he could obtain the help of the British naval commanders. So Robertson found his way to H.M.S. *Victory*, the flagship of Admiral Saumarez in the Baltic, and told his story. The Admiral at once saw that the matter was urgent, and sent a squadron under Keats, his second in command, to communicate with Romana.

It was necessary to maintain the utmost secrecy while arranging for all the Spanish garrisons to concentrate for embarkation, in defiance of French and Danes. Romana and Keats worked in concert, but the operation was extremely difficult. The various garrisons in Jutland were to seize vessels in the different harbours, and come to the island of Funen, where Romana had occupied the town of Nyborg on the Great Belt. Here Admiral Keats waited with his ships.

All went well. The Jutland garrisons arrived and were embarked, in spite of some opposition from two Danish gunboats. The Spanish troops were taken to Gottenburg, where transports had been provided to convey them to their native country. They were landed at Santander.

The Marquis de la Romana himself went to London to confer with the British Government. He accompanied Mr. Hookham Frere to Spain, who had been accredited as Envoy to the Central Junta. Both arrived at Coruña on October 20, 1808, and Romana proceeded to take command of the Spanish forces in Galicia. Here the indefatigable Majorcan maintained an unequal contest with Soult and Ney. Routed in February 1809 at Monterey, he still kept the field, aroused the whole country by his proclamations and by the sight of his patriotic zeal, and in the following April captured the French garrison at Villa Franca.

Finding that Ney was collecting a great force to annihilate him, Romana crossed the mountains at the passes of Cienfuegos and marched into the Asturias. Leaving his army at Navia de Suara, the general went on to Oviedo to organise the civil government of the province. Ney then conceived a plan of surprising the troops at Navia de Suara and securing the person of Romana. He sent Kellermann by forced marches to Oviedo, but the Marquis was not to be caught. He galloped down to the port of Gijon with his staff and returned by sea to Galicia. His troops also retreated safely across the mountains.

In 1809 Romana was appointed to be a member of the Central Junta at Seville, and he bade farewell to his faithful troops, who had escaped with him from Denmark and shared all his desperate campaigning work in Galicia. As a member of the Central Junta the Marquis drew up a very able State paper for the better government of the country, which had the concurrence both of Mr. Frere and of his successor, Lord Wellesley. In January 1810 he was appointed to command the Spanish army in Estremadura, where he did excellent service and saved Badajos at least for the time. When Lord Wellington retreated behind the lines of Torres Vedras, Romana joined him with four thousand men, and they then first became acquainted.

Wellington concerted his plans with Romana, who was, in the ensuing campaign, to keep open communications with Badajos, behind the Gevora. The Marquis began his march thither, but died very suddenly of heart-disease on January 23, 1811. A small edition of Pindar was found in his pocket. His death was most disastrous, for the troops had no confidence in his successor, and Badajos was lost.

Wellington appreciated the great qualities of this illustrious Majorcan soldier. He recorded his sense of Romana's services in the following tribute to his memory: 'In Romana the Spanish army has lost its brightest ornament, his country their most upright patriot, and the world the most strenuous and zealous defender of the cause in which we are engaged. I shall always acknowledge with gratitude the assistance which I received from him, as well by his operations as by his counsel, since he had been joined with this army.'[26] The body of the great Majorcan was conveyed to his native island. The funeral took place with all possible solemnity on June 4, 1811, and a monument was voted by the Cortes.

The monument is on the east wall of one of the northern side-chapels in the cathedral. The recumbent figure of the Marquis of Romana rests on a tomb, all in white marble, and beside it is another figure, pointing upwards, supposed to be the Duke of Wellington. Below there is a bas-relief with Romana and Admiral Keats superintending the embarkation of Spanish troops and baggage at Nyborg, in the island of Funen.

The son of the great general, also named Pedro, succeeded as fourth Marquis of Romana, and married Doña Tomas Alvarez de Toledo y Palafox, Duchess of Montalto. He died in 1848, and was succeeded by Don Pedro Caro, the fifth Marquis, who married a Hungarian lady of rank, Isabel Szechenyi Zichy-Ferraris. She built the castle of Bendinat, as has already been mentioned; but afterwards disposed of all the Caro property in Majorca, and went to Madrid, where her son, the present and sixth Marquis of La Romana, now resides.

Every visitor to Palma should go to the tomb of the illustrious Majorcan, whose splendid career was so closely connected with most interesting episodes in English history. Romana was the intimate friend of Hookham Frere, one of the most distinguished among the diplomatists and men of letters of the last century; and he won the esteem and friendship of the great Duke of Wellington.

At the same time that the corrupt government of Godoy sent the Marquis of Romana and fourteen thousand patriotic soldiers to Denmark, an equally illustrious man was sent a prisoner to Majorca. Jovellanos is connected with the island, not as a native, but as one whose iniquitous imprisonment won for him the warm sympathy of the islanders.

Gaspar Melchior de Jovellanos was born at Gijon, the chief seaport of the Asturias, in 1744, and received a liberal education. After a close study of civil and canon law, he became a judge at Seville, and afterwards at Madrid. He was a student of political economy and history, while he also attained eminence as a poet. His prose writings proved him to be a philosophical statesman as well as a very able man of letters. His liberal views were not acceptable to the favourite of Charles IV., and Jovellanos was sent into exile in his native province of Asturias. In 1797 he was recalled and became Minister of Justice. But Godoy still hated his enlightened opinions, and in the following year he was again banished to the Asturias.

The wretched favourite of Charles IV. was not yet satisfied. In 1801, in violation of law and decency, the illustrious statesman was seized in his bed, hurried across Spain like a common criminal, and sent a prisoner to Majorca. At first he was confined in the Cartuja at Valdemosa, but after a year he was removed to a prison in the castle of Belver. He was treated with such rigour that almost all communication with the outer world was cut off.

Latterly he was allowed to receive papers, and was even enabled to make researches in the archives. We are indebted to Jovellanos for an excellent account of the building of the cathedral and for learned pamphlets on the 'Lonja' and on the castle of Belver.

At last came the fall of the favourite and the abdication of Charles IV. This at once led to the liberation of Jovellanos, who was welcomed back and received the admiration of his countrymen for his great services and for the calm patience with which he had endured his unjust sufferings. He represented Asturias in the Central Junta at Seville, and on its dissolution he returned to his home in the hope that he would be allowed to end his days in peace. He was at Gijon, his native town, when the French made the sudden incursion into the Asturias in the hope of capturing the Marquis of Romana. He sought safety on board a small vessel, which landed him at the little port of Vega. There he died on November 27, 1811, at the age of fifty-seven. Ticknor, who was well acquainted with the writings of Jovellanos, wrote of him that 'he left behind him few men, in any country, of a greater elevation of mind, and fewer still of a purer or more irreproachable character.'[27]

The old castle of Belver continued to be misused during the dark times of recent Spanish history for the imprisonment of Carlist and other political victims. But the interesting building is now declared to be 'patrimonio real,' is inhabited by courteous and intelligent guardians, and is pen to the public.

In the gloomy vaulted room where Jovellanos was imprisoned for six years his island admirers have put up a marble tablet recording the fact and commemorative of his patriotic virtues.

CHAPTER XVIII
CONCLUSION

The story of Majorca has, in the course of its detailed narration, included attempts to describe the scenery of various localities of the island, the capital in ancient times, the mountains and caves, the towns and country houses. With the conclusion of the story we turn to the island as it is at present. We find areas of forest-covered mountains, which are calculated to contain 25,000 acres of pines, 12,000 acres of ilex, and 2,000 of carob-trees; at least, this was the calculation twenty years ago. The best account of the geology of these mountains will be found in the work of M. Hermite.[28]

Turning to the trees grown to support the people in the fertile plains, the same authority gives an area of 50,000 acres as covered by vines and 33,000 by almond-trees, besides apricots. The olives cover 86,000 acres—70,000 in the mountains, and the rest for the most part near their bases. The flora of the island is abundant and beautiful; and there is an excellent book on the subject by Don Francisco Barcelo y Combis.[29]

The people are the descendants of men who fought with En Jayme, increased by a certain amount of immigration—Catalans who speak a dialect of the Catalan language among themselves, but who nearly all understand Spanish. Among the upper classes the names of Moncada or Togores, Sureda, Cotoner, Fortuñy, Zaforteza, Despuig, Torrellas, Truyolls, Villalonga, are as prominent now as they were six hundred years ago and have been ever since. After a visitor has seen the cathedral and churches, the Lonja with its slender pillars, and the handsome Casa Consistorial with its frescoes and portraits of Majorcan worthies, nothing can be more interesting than to saunter through the streets and look at the old palaces of the nobility, with their quaint architecture, coats of arms, and picturesque courtyards. In front of the 'Mercado' is the great palace of the Burgues Zaforteza family. In a street of the same name is the Montenegro palace. In the narrow Fortuñy Street there is an ancient house with the name of Priamo Villalonga carved over the lintel of the door. Here lived the gallant defender of the royal castle against the rebels in 1522. The Villalongas are no longer there, having moved to a more modern abode in another part of the town. In nearly every street there is a palace or some other building which is interesting either for its architecture or its associations.

Among the leading people of Palma the name of Don Bartolomé Bosch y Cerda, His Britannic Majesty's Vice-Consul, cannot be overlooked, for his courtesy and kindness and his thorough knowledge of the island have largely increased the pleasure derived by many visitors from a sojourn in Majorca.

The best-known visitor—if His Highness ought not rather to be called a resident—was the Archduke Luis Salvator, whose magnificent monograph of the Balearic Islands is well known. Miramar has been mentioned as the abode of King Sancho, and afterwards as the place where Raimondo Lulio founded his college. But it is better known as the spot which the Archduke turned into an earthly paradise. He rebuilt the house which existed on the site of the former convent, laid out the lovely garden, and constructed roads and paths. He filled the house with old Majorcan furniture and Majolica ware, some of it with the metallic lustre for the manufacture of which the island was once famous. The Archduke also restored a little chapel in the garden, which contains an ancient picture of Raimondo Lulio. But it is now more than twelve years since the Archduke has visited the island.

The Majorcans excel as masons and carpenters. The mole, which forms the harbour, is as fine a piece of masonry work as is to be found in the Mediterranean. All the ashlar work of public buildings is remarkable for the fineness and exactness of the points of junction; and the vaulting, especially in the churches, displays no small mechanical skill, and even genius. Carpenters' work is equally good; and it is interesting to see them at work, with their shops open to the streets. There are many factories in the island; and while one member of a family works on a farm, others at trades, the rest can get employment in factories. All help, and the cottage in which the family lives generally has a small garden of flowers and vegetables. All the people are decently dressed and shod and have sufficient food. The Majorcans are certainly a handsome race, the men strongly built and well set up, the young women comely and graceful.

There are no beggars, except a few cripples. Begging or seeking presents is not the habit of the people. If boys are offered small change received in a shop they will generally refuse it, saying that they have done nothing for it. The cathedral carpenter sent his boy up a tree, at the request of a stranger, to get a leaf, and he was given a shilling for want of change. Some time afterwards the same stranger was passing, and the carpenter came out with the difference between a shilling and a *peseta*, saying he thought that the present was intended to be a *peseta* and not a shilling. Information respecting land tenures, mode of cultivation, exports, and other statistics will be found in Mr. Bidwell's 'Balearic Islands.'[30]

The story of Majorca is necessarily very closely connected with the general history of Aragon and its various dependencies. It is full of chivalrous deeds and wonderful adventures, as well as of evidence of those more solid and steady efforts which indicate fine qualities in a race. Thus, in the course of centuries, the existing islanders have been formed, and they are very much what might have been expected from their history. It is a history which should have a place in the study of European progress and development; for, small though the island is, the Majorcans have been in the forefront during the Middle Ages, and even in later times, alike as men of the sword and men of the pen. A knowledge of the island's story will furnish a number of historical associations which will, as it were, clothe the beautiful scenery with living interest. It thus appeals alike to the student who remains at home and to the traveller who visits the island.

It seems desirable to conclude with some information for the latter class of readers respecting accommodation at Palma. The hotel, which was opened a few years ago by Señor Albareda, faces the old church of St. Nicholas and the Zaforteza palace; while the avenue called the 'Rambla' is on one hand, and the 'Paseo del Borne,' leading to the port, on the other. It possesses every comfort and convenience, is admirably managed, and has a well-informed and most obliging landlord. This 'Grand Hotel' has a pleasant annex in the country, at Porto Pi, and the hotel in the beautiful valley of Soller is also comfortable and well managed. The visitor to Majorca is thus able to make himself acquainted with the lovely scenery, the history, and present condition of the island under the most advantageous conditions.

MAJORCA

PART II
MINORCA

CHAPTER I
MINORCA—ITS PREHISTORIC REMAINS— MAGO THE CARTHAGINIAN—SUCCESSIVE OCCUPATIONS

The sister island of Minorca is some twenty miles E.N.E. of Majorca, and is about the size of the Isle of Wight, twenty-one miles in length by eight broad. But its smaller size and more exposed situation deprive it of advantages enjoyed by its more favoured sister. Minorca is in the shape of an irregular parallelogram, lying W.N.W. to E.S.E., and has an area of 683 square kilometres. The island is divided into two distinct regions of almost equal extent by a line running east and west. The northern half is covered with hills, for the most part bare, with two culminating points. Near the centre of the island is 'Monte Toro,' rising in the form of a sugarloaf to a height of 1,150 feet. Farther west is the Monte de Santa Agueda, 850 feet high. The rock consists of slates, with strata generally much contorted and of Devonian age, but capped in some places by Jurassic rocks which contain fossils and numerous impressions of plants.

Owing to the frequent northerly gales, especially in the winter, the arboreal vegetation of the northern region, and indeed of the whole island, is scanty. There are some woods of ilex and Aleppo pines in sheltered places, and the shrub vegetation consists of myrtle, a *Phillirea* (wild olive?), and three species of *Erica*.

The southern region is more sheltered and more fertile. It consists of an undulating tableland cut by profound ravines and sloping from the hills to the southern coast, where it terminates in rocky cliffs. The formation is a good building limestone of Miocene age with nearly horizontal strata. In this southern region the shrubby vegetation consists of a buckthorn (*Rhamnus Alaternus*) and the *lentisco* (*Pistacia Lentiscus*). But there are few trees, and the ground is excessively stony. In the ravines the vegetation becomes richer and more varied.

There are no rivers or streams, and the people are entirely dependent on wells and cisterns for their supply of water. The rocks abound in caves, some natural, but many excavated in prehistoric times. There is one vast stalactitic cave near the western coast, with smaller branch caverns, and several other caves of the same kind on a smaller scale.

One of the principal features of interest in Minorca is the number of prehistoric remains scattered over the southern region. There are a few similar remains in Majorca, but they have been used almost entirely for building materials; and in Minorca they are far more numerous and less injured.

The primitive inhabitants appear to have been cave-dwellers. The buildings may have belonged to a later period. They have been described by several observers, notably by M. Emile Cartailhac in his 'Monuments primitifs des Iles Baléares';[31] but never more clearly, and with more competent knowledge of similar monuments in other parts of the world, than by Dr. Guillemard in his very able paper read before the Cambridge Antiquarian Society. Dr. Guillemard divides the Minorcan prehistoric buildings into four classes: (1) the so-called towns, (2) the *Naus* or ship-like edifices, (3) the *Taulas* or *Bilithons*, (4) the *Talayuts*.

The towns, really the size of small hamlets, are surrounded by a wall with a megalithic gateway, and sometimes with small towers on the walls, which consist of large blocks of limestone. Inside there are the remains of small square buildings, with underground low and narrow passages or caves.

The *Naus* is a building with a supposed resemblance to a ship, one end being pointed and the other square. There are only a few on the island. Cartailhac mentions nine. Their length is from twenty-five to forty feet, height fifteen to eighteen. The finest, called 'Nau d'Es Tudons,' is near Ciudadela. It consists of large blocks of stone dressed with a hammer. The entrance is three feet square, leading to a sort of vestibule, whence another door opens into the main chamber, which is supported by pillars down the middle. These edifices are carefully built, and were evidently the tombs of great men. The *Taulas* are two massive stones joined by a deep tenon and mortise and cut with remarkable care. The lower one is upright, and bears the upper one horizontally, like a table. They are in the centre of a building in the form of a semicircle forty feet across, the two ends being joined by a wall. Some twelve or fourteen *taulas* remain. They must almost certainly have been altars, or the main features of temples. These *taulas* appear to be closely allied to such edifices as Stonehenge or those at Avebury. In that case, they may be considered to date from about the same period, a date which has been ascertained astronomically by Sir Norman Lockyer—2000 B.C. The race of men who built them extended over Europe. They had dolichocephalic heads of average capacity, oval faces, aquiline noses, low foreheads, exactly like the skulls from the Basque provinces. They were not only spread over Europe, but established themselves in Mauritania (Morocco) and were probably the ancestors alike of the Guanches of Tenerife and the Baleares of these islands. The fourth class of prehistoric edifices consists of the *Talayuts*, so called from the Arabic 'Atalaya' or scout, hence watch-tower. Their height is usually not more than twenty feet. The largest, called 'Torre Llafuda,' is forty feet high. They are often forty feet in diameter at the base and six or seven feet less at the top. In 1818 Ramis gave a list of 195 of them, of which 142 were in fair condition. Since that time many have been used for limekilns or as quarries in building houses. They are all built of the rough vesicular limestone of the surrounding land,

and the stones are generally roughly dressed and laid in courses. The walls are of enormous thickness, with a circular chamber in the centre, supported by a pillar of massive stones. There is usually a doorway on the south side.

Their object has been a puzzle. They were not watch-towers from the positions of many of them; not fortresses, not dwellings, not temples, not tombs, for no bones are found. I believe that Dr. Guillemard, whose excellent descriptions of the Minorcan prehistoric remains I have been quoting, has hit upon the right solution. The fields are covered with stones, and one of the principal occupations of the husbandman is to clear the stones off the cultivable land. In modern times they make stone walls, for something has to be done with them. Dr. Guillemard holds that the *talayuts* are the stones cleared from the fields by the ancient people. They built these very solid towers with them, which served to house pigs and sheep at night; perhaps also as a look-out place, where their positions would serve such a purpose. But clearing the fields of stones was the primary object.

The Minorcan builders of stone temples, tombs, and dwellings, and pilers up of stones were prehistoric beyond any doubt, and may have worked and worshipped them four thousand years ago. The Phœnicians probably found their descendants on the island, and they became subject to the Semitic traders and their Carthaginian offshoots, who held the Balearic Islands while they were dominant in Spain. Minorca was best known as possessing the most capacious and safest harbour in the Mediterranean, and its name of Port Mahon makes the giver of that name an important factor in the story of the island.Mago was the youngest son of Hamilcar Barca, and when he first began to serve under his brother Hannibal in Italy, in B.C. 218, he must have been very young; but his capacity and fitness for command were soon realised by the great general. Mago was given command of the cavalry, and led his troops across the river Po, each man swimming by the side of his horse. Mago did distinguished service at the battle of Trebia, and was by his brother's side at Cannæ. He was then detached to reduce Samnium and the Bruttii. In about B.C. 212 he was sent to reinforce his other brother, Hasdrubal, in Spain. It was a losing cause, for the Carthaginians vainly opposed the victorious career of Scipio. The brothers resisted long. At last they were hopelessly defeated by Scipio at a place called Silpia, apparently in the Sierra Morena. Mago long held out at Gades. Here he received orders to collect troops and ships, and to make a diversion by landing at Genoa and transferring the seat of war to Italy. Having diligently assembled troops and the means of transport, he left Spain for ever and made sail, shaping a course, in compliance with his instructions, from Carthage. Mago wintered in the splendid harbour at the eastern end of Minorca, which has ever since borne his name—Portus Magonis, corrupted into Port Mahon.Eventually he landed his army at Genoa, but was defeated by Quinctilius Varro in a battle in Liguria, when he was severely wounded. Hannibal and Mago were recalled from Italy B.C. 203, and the younger brother died of his wounds on the voyage to Carthage, according to Livy. He was probably not more than thirty-two years of age. The name of this enterprising Carthaginian is immortalised in that of the harbour where he wintered, and in those of an English earl's second title and of a Spanish dukedom.During their occupation the Carthaginians had built three towns: the Portus Magonis; the town at the west end of the island, called Jamno, the modern Ciudadela; and one in the interior. In B.C. 121 Metellus arrived with his fleet, and the Balearic Islands passed under the dominion of Rome. For more than five hundred years the islands formed part of the Roman Empire, Minorca always sharing the fate of her larger and more important sister. These huge gaps in history leave everything to conjecture. They may have been a time of peace and prosperity, or they may have been a period of grinding oppression. The people were probably still the descendants of the prehistoric builders. Certainly no great event happened, or it would have been recorded. On the decay of Roman power, in the days of Honorius, the Balearic Islands are said to have been occupied for a time by the Vandals, from A.D. 426. It is assumed that the islands formed part of the kingdom of the Spanish Visigoths; but all that may have happened in that long period is buried in oblivion. We only know that Christianity had been introduced, and that at the Council of Toledo, celebrated in the year 675 A.D., there were bishops of the Balearic Isles, dating for at least two hundred years back, for Severo was Bishop of Minorca in 423.Before the commencement of the ninth century the islands had fallen entirely into the hands of the Moors, and formed part of the empire of the Omeyad Khâlifas of Cordova, Minorca continuing through all the long period of Moorish domination to share the fate of the larger island. The aboriginal inhabitants must have entirely disappeared, giving place to immigrants from Africa and Muhammadan Spain, chiefly Arabs and Berbers. Minorca seems to have been ruled during a long period by a Moorish family, son succeeding father, with a title which the Spaniards called Almojarife. We have already seen how, after the conquest of Majorca, King Jayme secured the submission of the Minorcan Moors by a stratagem.[32] The great king, however, dealt very leniently with the smaller island. The government of Minorca was confirmed to the Almojarife and his family on condition of loyalty to the Aragonese overlord and payment of tribute. This arrangement continued until the usurpation of young Alfonso III., a very different man from his illustrious grandfather. The Moors were established in Minorca for nearly four centuries; but, by the use of ruthless methods, it is not difficult to extirpate a whole population and to substitute another in so small an island.

CHAPTER II
CONQUEST OF MINORCA BY ALFONSO III.—
THE BARBARY PIRATES

The young King Alfonso III. of Aragon, having usurped the government of Majorca, as has been related in the story of that island,[33] came to a sudden determination to drive the Moors out of Minorca. He made a pretext that the Almojarife had thwarted his father's designs on the coast of Barbary by giving early information to his co-religionists. Alfonso also said that when his uncle's dominions were restored to him, the acquisition of Minorca would make up for the temporary deprivation. This hopeful young king had not begun well. He was unjust, wayward, and sometimes cruel. He acted on the spur of the moment. Had he lived, the promised son-in-law of the great King Edward of England might have become a more stable and right-minded prince. At this time he cared very little for a pretext in making war, and his resolutions were very hastily formed.

The consequence was that he chose the stormiest period of the winter for his expedition, sending to his brother Fadrique, in Sicily, to supply him with forty well-armed galleys. He then assembled the nobles of his kingdom at Tarragona, and was granted five hundred cavalry and a large army of *almogavares*.[34] The fleet of armed ships and transports numbered 120 sail. En Pedro Cornel was appointed general of the forces, and knights of the families of Luna, Entenza, Anglesola accompanied the King. Garcia Gorcas de Aracuri of Aragon and Acart de Mur of Catalonia were masters of the camp.

The terrible news reached the Almojarife[35] of Minorca. His consternation was great, for the danger was imminent. The impulsive young king cared less than nothing for the written grant given by En Jayme to the Moorish chief. The Almojarife sent to Barbary to entreat for help from the chiefs of Bugia, Bona, Tremecen, and Constantia. In a short time 900 cavalry and 5,000 foot soldiers arrived from Africa, which would enable the Moors to face their enemies with a respectable force.

The King of Aragon left Salou with his fleet, arriving at Majorca on December 2, 1285, where he passed Christmas. Muntaner tells us that the cold of that winter was intense, and that a man might as well have been in the frozen steppes of the Don. The hands of some of the oarsmen were frostbitten, and the troops suffered from the severity of the winter.

After the Christmas festivities were over, the King ordered the fleet to make sail in the worst possible weather. The ships were scarcely clear of the land when a furious gale sprang up and scattered the fleet. Alfonso arrived at Port Mahon with only twenty galleys, and occupied one of the rocky islands in the harbour, waiting for the rest of his forces.

The Moors were ready to receive him. They had a large army, composed partly of the auxiliaries sent from Africa and partly of natives of the island. Seeing them drawn up in battle array, the impetuous young King resolved to attack them without waiting for reinforcements. He had a few companies of *almogavares* and four hundred horse. A very desperate and well-contested battle was the result. Alfonso was in the thick of the fight, giving many proofs of valour and dexterity as a swordsman. In spite of the great inferiority in numbers, the Catalans were victorious, the Moors retreating in confusion to a hill which, owing to the great slaughter, received the name of 'El Degollador.' The battlefield was situated on a plain a little to the westward of the present castle of San Felipe.

A day or two afterwards there was another fight, owing to the conduct of a young knight named Berenguer de Tornamira, who, to show his own valour, attacked the Moors without orders with a small force. If succour had not been promptly despatched he would certainly have been overwhelmed. As it was, the Moors were driven back. The Almojarife then took refuge, with the remnant of his forces, in the castle on Mount Santa Agueda. Alfonso, always hasty and violent, ordered Tornamira's head to be cut off; but he afterwards yielded to the prayers and remonstrances of his nobles and consented to spare the young knight's life. The losses in these two battles were very heavy, especially on the side of the Moors. By this time the rest of the fleet, with troops on board, had arrived at Port Mahon.

Alfonso then advanced to the castle of Santa Agueda, and made preparations for a siege; but the Almojarife saw that all hope was gone, and sent four of his principal ministers to ask for the acceptance of the terms he offered. They were that he would surrender the castle and the whole island if he and his people were provided with shipping to proceed to Barbary, paying 7-1/2 *doblas* a head for every Moorish man or woman that embarked. The Almojarife also asked to be allowed to take his books, clothes, and fifty swords. The ship was to take him to Ceuta or some other port in Africa. The King consented to the terms, and his favourite, Blasco Jimenes de Ayerba, was instructed to make the necessary arrangement. There was a Genoese vessel at Port Mahon, which was hired and supplied with provisions, and the unfortunate chief, with his family and about a hundred other people who were able to pay the ransom, embarked. Whether the ship went down in a gale of wind, or whether there was foul play, no one will ever know. It is certain that she never was heard of again. The story of Carbonell that the unfortunate fugitives were thrown overboard by order of the King, after paying their ransoms, need not be believed.

The rest of the population was at the mercy of the conquerors, to the number of about twenty thousand. They were either forced to work at the new buildings ordered to be erected, or sent to Sicily and Barcelona to be sold as slaves.

The date of the capitulation was January 17, 1288, St. Anthony's Day, which was ever afterwards kept as a holiday, with processions and other festivities. Alfonso remained in Minorca until the following March, leaving orders for a town to be built, with a fortified wall, at Port Mahon. He died three years afterwards at Barcelona, aged twenty-seven.

Don Juan Ramis y Ramis, the chronicler of Minorca, recorded the prowess of the young King and the conquest of the island in a poem entitled 'Alonsiada.'

Pedro de Lesbia, a native of Valencia, was left as the first Christian Procurator-General of Minorca. The whole Moorish population appears to have been rooted out of the island and replaced by Catalan settlers. Ciudadela, at the western end, became the capital, as it was in Moorish times; while Port Mahon was the principal commercial port.

In a small island like Minorca a population could soon be extirpated by ruthless invaders without pity or remorse and actuated by unreasoning bigotry. Their cruelties were not only condoned but encouraged by their priests. It is a revolting picture. There was an industrious and happy people, engaged in cultivating a not very grateful soil, which needed much toil and no little skill to induce it to yield harvests sufficient for the wants of a frugal population. In homes endeared to them by centuries of occupation, and surrounded by their wives and children, they were living in peace and comparative prosperity, and enjoying the hard-earned fruits of their toil. The land tax, paid in kind, was the regular source of revenue in all Muhammadan countries. In Minorca the Almojarife, or collector, appears to have been the hereditary chief of the island. Suddenly, like a bolt from the blue, in a few days total destruction came upon them. Thousands were killed, all their chief men with their families disappeared, all their property was seized, wives were torn from husbands, children from parents, and sold into slavery.

Turning away from the horrors of this scene of cruelty and wrong, we may assume an interval of confusion, and then the farms and villages of the Moors are occupied by Catalan families equally industrious and hard-working. The Christians were exposed to heavier exactions and suffered under a less enlightened rule, so that perhaps we should give them even greater credit than their predecessors for the way in which they extracted the means of supporting themselves and their families from the stony fields.

Minorca continued to share the fortunes of the larger island under her own kings, under the Kings of Aragon, and under the Austrian dynasty of Spain.

The form of government was the same as that granted to Majorca by En Jayme.

The smaller island suffered equally with Majorca from the raids of Barbary pirates, who carried off many unfortunate people into slavery. All the islanders rejoiced at the campaign against Tunis, led by the Emperor Charles V. in person, who liberated several thousands of Christian slaves in 1535. Yet the piracies did not cease, or only for a time. Barbarossa, the piratical leader, undeterred by the fall of Tunis, fitted out a fleet of eleven galleys and made sail for the Balearic Islands. His fleet entered Port Mahon with Christian banners flying, to deceive the soldiers in the fort and the inhabitants, who were completely taken in. Bells were rung and guns fired in honour of what was supposed to be a part of the Emperor's fleet. A boat with some Franciscan friars approached the galleys and discovered the mistake. They pulled back to the shore, raised a warning, and the gates of the town were closed.

Barbarossa landed 2,500 Moors and some guns, with which he battered the walls of the town and made a breach. His assault was, however, repulsed. The people of Ciudadela assembled three hundred men, but seeing that the enemy was so powerful they did not venture upon an attack at first. They sent a messenger to warn the besieged that they should be ready to make a sortie when the relief approached. Then most of the three hundred advanced, and occupied the attention of the enemy while the besieged hastily repaired the breaches in the walls. A second assault was gallantly repulsed, and the pirate chief began to feel rather insecure at Port Mahon, expecting the return of the Emperor's fleet from Tunis.

Fortunately for Barbarossa, the besieged lost heart and surrendered the town to him on terms which he never dreamt of keeping. He made slaves of eight hundred of the inhabitants. The churches were pillaged and profaned. The Guardian of San Francisco had partaken of the Sacrament to save the Host from profanation. The Moors entered and seized all the valuables, but did not find the Host in the pyx. Barbarossa asked where it was, and when the Franciscan replied that he had eaten it to preserve it from profanation, he was ordered out for execution and suffered death with two other friars.

This was in the year 1536. The Governor of the island had remained at Ciudadela, and when six citizens arrived from Port Mahon, who had been released by Barbarossa because they advised the surrender, the Governor ordered them to be put to death. Barbarossa and his Moors evacuated Port Mahon and departed with his plunder and with many wretched people to be sold into slavery. The Emperor was greatly distressed at these repeated acts of piracy, and in 1541 he fitted out a second expedition, this time against Algiers. Again he led the expedition in person; but it was a failure owing to the furious gales and deluges of rain.

The islands were kept in a constant state of alarm. In 1558 a Turkish fleet of 140 vessels hove in sight. Ciudadela and Port Mahon had been put in the best possible posture of defence, when fifteen thousand Turks were landed, under a leader named Mustapha. Having occupied the open country, they laid siege to Ciudadela, which was held by a garrison of seven hundred men. A battery of artillery was planted against the walls, and, after making a breach, three assaults were delivered and gallantly repulsed. The besieged Minorcans were resolved to defend the place to the death, and they would have done so if it had not been for a disastrous accident. The magazine caught fire and all their powder was destroyed. The men proposed to their leaders, Arquimbau, the Lieutenant-Governor, and Captain Noyet, to attempt to fight their way to Port Mahon. They came out, the men of Alayor and Mercadal leading, women and children in the centre, and the rest of the garrison bringing up the rear, under Arquimbau. The Turks attacked them furiously, and only 150 got back into the town. On July 10 another assault was delivered, and at last the place was taken. Many of the besieged were killed in cold blood, and the rest were carried off to be sold as slaves. On the same day the Turks embarked and made sail.

The Viceroy, Don Guillermo Rocafull, was not in the island. He returned at once and proceeded to repair the fortifications of Ciudadela, bringing several families to re-people the place from Majorca and Valencia. The castle of San Felipe at Port Mahon was also repaired and strengthened.

The piracies continued until well into the eighteenth century, and kept the people in a constant state of terror and alarm; but confidence slowly returned, and Minorca had long been free from actual invasion when the War of the Succession broke out, after the death of Charles II., the last of the Austrian Kings of Spain.

CHAPTER III
BRITISH OCCUPATION OF MINORCA.

The people of Spain had long been misgoverned, impoverished, and oppressed when the last king of the House of Austria died and left the War of Succession as a legacy to his subjects.

The descendant of Maria Teresa, sister of Charles II. and wife of Louis XIV. of France, would have had the best right if her marriage had not been allowed on condition of the most solemn renunciation of the crown of Spain for the offspring of it. The next heir was the Emperor Leopold I., descended from a sister of Philip IV. of Spain, the father of Charles II. He resigned his claim to his second son, the Archduke Charles. Strongly in favour of the Austrian claim, the unhappy King was forced by priestly threats on his deathbed to sign a will declaring Philip, Duke of Anjou, grandson of Louis XIV. and Maria Teresa, to be heir to the Spanish monarchy. Philip was then seventeen. The Archduke Charles was fifteen.

Louis XIV. was strictly pledged to the Governments of England and Holland not to allow his grandson to succeed. In February 1701, in defiance of this solemn compact, Philip was sent to Madrid and proclaimed as Philip V. Castille acknowledged him. Aragon, Catalonia, and the Balearic Islands declared for the Archduke Charles as Charles III. He was supported by England, Holland, Portugal, Savoy, and the Empire. War was declared on May 15, 1702, and the War of the Spanish Succession commenced. In March 1704 Charles III. arrived at Lisbon with four thousand Dutch and eight thousand English troops, where he was joined by Don Juan Henriquez, Admiral of Castille, one of the greatest of the Spanish nobles. On August 3 Gibraltar was taken, and garrisoned with two thousand men, the Prince of Hesse Darmstadt being the first Governor. Charles III. then proceeded to Barcelona, the almost impregnable castle of Monjuich having previously been captured by the Earl of Peterborough. Amidst great rejoicings Charles made his public entry on October 23, 1705. Peterborough entered Valencia in triumph on February 4, 1706, and Majorca declared for King Charles.

General Stanhope was appointed Envoy Extraordinary to King Charles and sent out in command of reinforcements. He was a grandson of the first Earl of Chesterfield and son of Alexander Stanhope, who was Ambassador at Madrid in the time of Charles II. Having passed his youth in his father's house, he was well acquainted with Spanish and with the feelings of the people. He learnt the art of war under Marlborough.

The disastrous battle of Almanza was fought in April 1707, and for some time the cause of King Charles seemed almost hopeless. The Duke of

Berwick entered Valencia and conquered Aragon, the French claimant, Philip, abolishing all its provincial privileges; while General Stanhope was reduced to a strictly defensive system. King Charles's base was the east coast of Spain and the Mediterranean Sea. The English fleet was therefore of the utmost importance, and it became very urgent that the ships should remain out, instead of returning home for the winter. But, although Majorca was for Charles, the harbour of Port Mahon was still occupied by French and Spanish troops for Philip.

Stanhope, with his German colleague Staremburg, after several weeks of skilful but desultory manœuvres, obliged the French army to retreat from Tortosa, to which place the enemy had advanced. In August of the same year, 1707, Admiral Leake with the British fleet took Cagliari and secured the island of Sardinia for King Charles. But the most important enterprise was the capture of Minorca with its excellent harbour.

The Duke of Marlborough wrote to General Stanhope saying: 'I am so entirely convinced that nothing can be done effectually without the fleet, that I conjure you, if possible, to take Port Mahon.' Lord Godolphin sent out instructions to the same effect, which reached Stanhope when he was encamped at Cervera with Marshal Staremburg, at the close of the campaign against the French.

Stanhope immediately set out for Barcelona in pursuance of his instructions, but few men could be spared for the enterprise. Fortunately, Charles was fully alive to its great importance. Admiral Sir John Leake was still off Sardinia with the bulk of the fleet. There were, however, six men-of-war at Barcelona; but some of the captains hesitated to take any responsibility. The two who supported the General were his brother Philip of the *Milford*, and Trevanion of the *York*.

Stanhope forced their hands by actually embarking in some transports the troops he had been able to collect, and announcing his intention of proceeding at once to Majorca, there to await reinforcements. This made all the captains resolve to accompany him. One of the ships (the *Milford*) was commanded by the General's brother, Captain Philip Stanhope, and the two brothers sailed together. The force consisted of 1,200 British troops, including marines, 600 Portuguese, and the rest Spanish. The General wrote to Sir John Leake, who had just reduced Sardinia to obedience to Charles, sending a copy of the letter from Lord Godolphin, and entreating him to co-operate.

Sir John Leake was about to return with the Beet to England for the winter, leaving a squadron to guard the Portuguese coast. He, however, left Pula, near Cagliari, with the fleet on August 18, in compliance with General Stanhope's request, and arrived off Port Mahon on the 25th. He cruised off the island until September 14, when Stanhope arrived on board the *Milford*, the transports following on October 3.

Stanhope's plan was to land at once and lay siege to the castle of San Felipe. Measures were accordingly arranged with the Admiral, who lent all the marines and guns that could be spared. There were forty-two guns and thirteen mortars. A spot was selected about two miles from the castle to the south-west, and the troops were landed. All the inhabitants received them joyfully, declaring for King Charles; and the magistrates of Mahon came and delivered up the keys of their city. On the 7th the *Dunkirk*, *Centurion*, and *York* were anchored near the south-east point of the island, to cover the landing of the heavy guns. This was a service of great difficulty, for the only place for landing them was in a creek within half gunshot of the enemy's batteries. Nevertheless it was attempted that very evening, and effected with little loss. The country was found to be rocky and without roads, and the beasts of burden that could be obtained were so few that it was twelve days before the guns could be got into position ready to commence the attack.

On the 8th the fleet, consisting of fifteen sail of the line, under the command of Sir John Leake, sailed for England. The Admiral had lent the General as many marines as could possibly be spared, and supplied him with ammunition and some provisions. A squadron of seventeen sail was left off Port Mahon, under the command of Sir Edward Whitaker, the hero of Gibraltar, to assist in the reduction of the castle of San Felipe.

Two ships, the *Dunkirk* (Captain Butler) and *Centurion* (Captain Fairborn), were detached to take possession of the castle and harbour of Fornelle, on the north coast of the island. The *Dunkirk* arrived two hours before the *Centurion*, and opened a heavy fire, which was returned with some effect; but when the *Centurion* also hove in sight, the garrison surrendered as prisoners of war. All the transports and bomb-vessels were then sent to Fornelle creek, having previously had no secure place to ride in.

On the 28th General Stanhope opened a battery of nine guns on two towers flanking an outer line, which the garrison of San Felipe had lately thrown up, beating them down and making some breaches in the connecting walls. This was not difficult, as the works had been hastily run up with loose stones. Brigadier Lane was stationed on the right with two battalions. Captain Philip Stanhope commanded the marines. Some of Wade's men entered a breach in the wall without orders, and as soon as he saw their advance he followed with all his men. Philip Stanhope led on his marines, and there was a general advance, the garrison, after a short resistance, abandoning all the outworks and retreating into the castle. Next morning the enemy commenced a parley, which was followed by their capitulation in the afternoon. They could have held out for a long time. A hundred pieces of ordnance were found in the castle, three thousand barrels of powder, and all things necessary for a long defence. The victory was dearly bought with the death of Captain Philip Stanhope, who fell mortally wounded. He was struck by a ball on the forehead as he was held up by two sailors to look over a wall seven feet high. He was interred in one of the vaults of the castle. The General wrote: 'The conquest has cost me very dear, but since Philip died in doing service to Her Majesty and his country, I shall think his life well bestowed, as I should my own.'

Ciudadela at once surrendered, and its garrison of a hundred men became prisoners of war. There was no resistance in any other part of the island. Stanhope wrote: 'A great part of our success in reducing this island is owing to the zeal and affection the people have for us, which is beyond expression.' Port Mahon was garrisoned by British marines, and the fortifications were strengthened by new works at a cost of about 60,000*l*. It was General Stanhope's idea that Minorca should be held as a sort of mortgage for the large sums advanced to King Charles.

A medal was struck at the Tower to commemorate the conquests of Sardinia and Minorca.

> *Obv.*: Bust of Queen Anne.
>
> *Rev.*: Victory holding a palm-branch in one hand, and the Union Jack in the other. Two islands appearing in the distance, 'SARDINIA ET BALEARIS MINOR CAPTÆ.'
>
> *Exergue*: MDCCVII.

Stanhope returned to his military duties in Spain. He was at Barcelona again on November 9. It is not necessary to follow the course of events. The death of the Emperor Joseph I. in 1711 opened the succession to his brother Charles; while his want of success and the animosity of the Castilians destroyed all chance of his succeeding to the crown of Spain. In fact, he became Emperor of Germany as Charles VI.

The Ministry of Harley and St. John opened negotiations for peace. The abandonment of the Catalans and Majorcans to their fate cast an indelible stain of infamy on the British Government. Queen Anne had several times pledged her royal word for the preservation of the lives and liberties of the Catalans. In consequence of those promises the Catalans had begun and maintained an insurrection. Yet no stipulation was made in the treaty, and St. John had the effrontery to announce that 'it is not for the interests of England to preserve the Catalan liberties.'

On April 11, 1713, the Peace of Utrecht was signed, the Emperor Charles refusing to be a party to it. The French Prince was acknowledged as King of Spain, being Philip V. of that country, but resigning any right of succession to the French crown. The Duke of Savoy was to have Sicily; Gibraltar and Minorca were ceded to England; the Netherlands, Naples, Milan, and Sardinia to the Emperor. Lord Stanhope, the descendant of the conqueror of Minorca, has pleaded with some truth that, whilst the glories of the war belong to the whole British people, the disgrace of the peace, the unworthy result of such great achievements, rests on a small knot of factious politicians.

Their beloved King Charles, now Emperor of Germany, must be acquitted of blame as regards the Catalans and Majorcans. He was powerless. Writing to General Stanhope, he said: 'Knowing as I do your goodness of heart, I am persuaded that you and your friends will compassionate the fidelity, firmness, and misfortune of my poor Catalans. No difficulties, no dangers, no temptations could shake their generous loyalty. All this pierces my heart. I leave you to judge whether it is in my power to aid them without a naval force. I doubt not that you will consider the dreadful state to which they have been reduced by the evil-minded men of your country, contrary to the most solemn and repeated engagements.'

Catalonia and Majorca were abandoned to the mean vengeance of Philip. Minorca was more fortunate in becoming a British possession. In 1717 the conqueror of Minorca was created Viscount Stanhope of Mahon.

CHAPTER IV
MINORCA AS A BASE

Minorca was the chief gainer by the Peace of Utrecht. She secured many years of good government and freedom from oppression by her connection with her English friends. But England herself derived almost equal advantage. She had become a Mediterranean Power. She had Gibraltar, but it was necessary that she should also have a base within the inland sea where her ships could refit and her sailors could be refreshed; and this need was supplied in full measure by the splendid harbour of Port Mahon. The value of such a possession was experienced a very few years after the peace. The Emperor had sent an army into Hungary against the Turks, and Philip V. gave a solemn promise to the Pope that he would not undertake anything against the interests of the Emperor while he was engaged in so religious a cause. Yet, without regard to this promise and in defiance of the duties imposed upon him by the treaty of peace, he sent a fleet, with a land force of nine thousand men, from Barcelona, which seized upon the island of Sardinia in July 1717. His excuse was that King Charles had delivered up the towns in Catalonia and Majorca to the inhabitants, thus putting Philip to the trouble and expense of reducing those people to obedience.

In consequence of this aggression, the Powers made a treaty, called the Quadruple Alliance, by which the Emperor was to give up his claim to the crown of Spain, to receive Sicily from the Duke of Savoy, and to give him Sardinia in its place, with the title of King. Philip would not agree to this arrangement and continued his preparations for war, without any regard to the remonstrances of England and even of France. In this he was strongly influenced by his second wife and by his Minister, Cardinal Alberoni.

In order to prevent farther mischief in the Mediterranean a formidable fleet was got ready at Spithead, under the command of Admiral Sir George Byng, with orders to hinder and resist all attempts of Spain against Italy or Sicily. Byng sailed on June 25, 1718, with twenty ships of the line, two fire-ships, two bomb-ships, a hospital-ship, and a store-ship. Off Cape St. Vincent he sent a messenger, by way of Cadiz, to convey a letter to Lord Harrington, the British Envoy at Madrid, that the Spanish Government might be informed of the approach of the British fleet and of Byng's instructions.

The Envoy showed the letter to Cardinal Alberoni, who declared that his master would run all hazards rather than recall his fleet and troops, that the Spaniards would not be frightened, and that he had no fear of the result if Admiral Byng attacked them. The Envoy then requested his Eminence to look over a list of the British ships which he held in his hand. Alberoni snatched it and threw it on the ground, trampling on it in a great passion.

There was nothing more to be done with such a violent diplomatist. The British fleet entered the Mediterranean, and arrived at Port Mahon on July 23. Here the Admiral landed four regiments, and took the marines forming the old garrison to serve in the fleet. On August 1 the Admiral arrived at Naples, and conferred with Count Daun, the very popular Viceroy for the Emperor Charles VI. It was found that the Spaniards had landed an army in Sicily and were besieging Messina, and that there was a large Spanish fleet there, consisting of twenty-nine ships of the line and frigates, two being seventy-four-gun ships and eight with sixty guns.

On August 9 Sir George Byng with his formidable fleet arrived off Messina, and sent a letter to the Spanish General proposing to him that he should grant a cessation of hostilities for two months, to give time for the Powers to agree to a lasting peace, apprising him of his instructions in case of refusal. The Spaniard replied that he had no powers to treat, and that he would obey his orders, which were to seize Sicily for the King of Spain.

The Spanish fleet had weighed the day before, and was out of sight to the south. Byng went in chase, and before noon of the next day he came in sight of their twenty-seven men-of-war in order of battle. Don Antonio de Castaneta was the Admiral in command, and there were four rear-admirals, one of them an Irish renegade named Cammock. On sighting the English fleet they stood away, but still in order of battle. All that day and the succeeding night the English Admiral followed them. Early in the morning of the 11th one of the Spanish rear-admirals parted company with six frigates and all the galleys, bomb-vessels, and store-ships, standing for the Sicilian coast near Syracuse. Captain Walton of the *Canterbury*, with five vessels under his command, was detached in pursuit. Walton's report of his proceedings is a model of business-like brevity:

> 'SIR,—We have taken and destroyed all the Spanish ships and vessels which were upon the coast, the number as per margin.'

Admiral Byng continued the pursuit of the main fleet and came up with it off Cape Passaro. The *Orford* and *Grafton* were the foremost ships, and the Spaniards fired their stern chase guns. The order was given not to return the fire unless it was repeated. It was repeated, and the *Orford* promptly engaged the *Santa Rosa*, of sixty-four guns, and took her. Next the *San Carlos*, of sixty guns, struck to the *Kent*. The *Principe de Asturias*, with the flag of Rear-Admiral Chacon, was dealt with by the *Breda* and *Captain*. The Spanish Admiral's flagship, of seventy-four guns, made a running fight until 3 P.M., and then struck to the *Superbe*. Three other ships were taken. Sir George Byng employed the next few days refitting and repairing damages in the prizes. Nine of the Spanish ships escaped, thirteen were taken and became prizes, three were burnt, three sunk. Practically the Spanish fleet ceased to exist.

The value of Minorca as a base then became apparent. Rear-Admiral Cornwall was sent to Port Mahon with the ships that required repairs and all the prizes. On February 3, 1719, Sir George Byng went with the rest of the fleet to Port Mahon, to refresh the men and refit the ships. Returning to Naples in April, he found that Count Mercy had been appointed to the command of a German army to expel the Spaniards from Sicily. Mercy was a tall, soldier-like man, but excessively short-sighted. He had great strength of mind and body, was very ambitious, with an insatiable thirst for glory. He would have been a greater general if he had been endowed with a cooler temper. The task before him was a difficult one, although the English fleet gave him command of the sea. All things being ready, Sir George Byng sailed from Baia with eight men-of-war, escorting two hundred transports having on board 10,000 infantry and 3,500 horse. By the advice of the Savoyard Governor of Melazzo, the landing was effected on the coast about twenty miles to the westward of that fortress. Count Seckendorf was detached to reduce the Lipari Islands to the Emperor's obedience—an important matter, so as to keep the communications open between Naples and Sicily.

The Sicilian campaign commenced in May 1719, and there was some very severe fighting. Count Mercy found himself in considerable difficulties in the interior; for the natives were on the side of the Spaniards. He sent a message with an urgent request that Sir George Byng would come to him for a consultation. The Admiral did not hesitate. He set out with a strong escort, accompanied by his eldest son and Captain Matthews of the *Kent*. The road was strewn with the dead bodies of men and horses, and was very rugged, but they reached the Count's tent in the evening. A guard of honour was drawn up for the Admiral's reception, and one of the men was shot through the head at the door of the tent by a musket-ball from the enemy's camp. He fell dead at the Admiral's feet as he dismounted. Sir George found the Count very weak from a wound, the ball not having yet been extracted. But he was full of pluck, and desirous of again attacking the Spaniards in their strong position, though his officers advised a retreat to the coast. A council next day confirmed this opinion, and dwelt on the urgency of receiving reinforcements. Sir George therefore returned to the coast and immediately proceeded with two ships to Naples to represent the state of things to the Viceroy. He then returned to Sicily, where he found that Count Mercy had been disabled by an apoplectic seizure; but that his second in command had taken Taormina by surprise and advanced to Messina, where the siege was commenced on July 20. The town surrendered and Sir George Byng took his fleet into the harbour, but the citadel held out.

The Emperor had resolved to send troops from Milan, by way of Genoa, to reinforce Count Mercy, and, knowing the extreme slowness of the Germans, the Admiral resolved to superintend the business personally. On August 23 he returned to Naples, arriving at Genoa on September 7. He found everything extremely backward. After much worry and almost incredible trouble, what with persuasion and threats, he got seven thousand men on board the transports and brought them to Messina. The whole army was overjoyed to see a man who always brought them relief and succour. Count Mercy had returned from Reggio, but with the ball not yet extracted. He was delighted at the Admiral's success in bringing him help. It decided the fate of the citadel, which surrendered after a siege of ninety-one days. The Spanish General then fortified the almost impregnable position at Castro Giovanni; but Count Mercy and the Admiral thought it more important to occupy Palermo, and while operations for that purpose were being pushed forward the Spaniards offered to evacuate Sicily on terms.

Early in 1720 the news arrived that Philip V. had given up his ambitious projects and joined the Quadruple Alliance. Sicily and Sardinia were to be evacuated by the Spaniards within two months. During May and June the Spanish troops were embarked in transports at Termini and sent to Barcelona. The Duke of Savoy was then put into quiet possession of Sardinia. Thus the work was completed for the execution of which the British fleet under Sir George Byng had been sent to the Mediterranean. The English Admiral certainly deserves the highest credit. He was diligent in preparing his measures, attending to every detail himself. In action he was alike careful and energetic. His patience under the most trying circumstances was inexhaustible. He was most successful as a diplomatist, and at length he acquired such influence that he was looked to as an umpire in the numerous misunderstandings and disputes of rival commanders. Thus the service that was entrusted to him, a most harassing and difficult service, was performed with remarkable ability and complete success. On his return he was created Viscount Torrington, and in 1733 he died in harness as First Lord of the Admiralty.

Minorca played an unostentatious but very important part in this campaign. Without that base for refitting the ships and refreshing the men the difficulties of Admiral Byng would have been increased tenfold.

CHAPTER V
MINORCA UNDER BRITISH RULE

If the occupation of Minorca was very important to the British as a base for their fleet, it was an even greater blessing to the inhabitants. While the ancient rights and liberties of the Catalans and Majorcans were ruthlessly destroyed by their Bourbon conqueror, the Minorcans were treated very differently. Their religion, their form of civil government, their customs and traditions were all respected by the English, who came as friends rather than as masters. It will be interesting to glance over the condition of the island during the earlier years of British occupation.

Minorca was divided into five provinces, called *terminos*. At the eastern end was the *termino* of Mahon with the capital under British rule, and at the western the *termino* of Ciudadela, the ancient capital. Between them were the *terminos* of Alaior, Mercadal, and Fererias, each with its chief village of the same name. Mercadal included the greater part of the northern coast.

The principal feature of the island is the splendid harbour of Port Mahon, with deep water, and capable in former days of sheltering all the fleets of Europe. There are several small islands in the harbour, and on one the hospital was built when Sir John Jennings was Commander-in-Chief in the Mediterranean, 1711-13. The quarantine station was on another island. The picturesque town of Mahon, built entirely of freestone, rose up the side of a hill, with its great church and monasteries showing above the roofs of the houses. The streets were rocky and narrow, but the site was fresh and healthy. Along the waterside there was a long quay, one end being reserved for the navy and naval stores, and the other for trading vessels and merchandise.

At the entrance of the harbour is the castle of San Felipe, on a neck of land between Port Mahon and St. Stephen's Cove. The main fort consisted of four bastions connected by curtains, with a deep ditch hewn out of the solid rocks. Within the area there were the Governor's house, barracks, guard-room, and chapel. In the centre there was a pump to supply the troops with rain water from a large cistern. The whole rock is undermined with subterranean passages and chambers. A considerable suburb, including barracks and officers' quarters, rose up outside the castle. The plain beyond is stony and barren, but at the head of St. Stephen's Cove there is a *barranco* or ravine, bounded by rocks on either side, where there are fruit trees and garden vegetables of all kinds. These *barrancos* are the fertile and fruit-yielding parts of the island. Originally long creeks penetrating into the land from the sea, they have been gradually filled with rich soil by floods from the hills on the north side, until they were raised above the sea level. There is no tide to carry off the deposits brought down from the hills. At the upper end of the harbour there is another extensive *barranco*, known as the gardens of San Juan, which was the principal source of supply of vegetables for Mahon. A few miles farther north is the *albufera*, or salt lake, separated from the sea by a sand-spit, and abounding in fish; and still farther to the north are the harbour and beautiful valley of Adaia. Wild pigeons and rabbits frequent the rocky cliffs and islands on the coast.

The interior of the island is barren and stony, except for the *barrancos*. Alaior was a tolerably well-built town on an eminence; but Mercadal and Fererias are only wretched villages. The north coast is deeply indented, and Port Fornelle is a large harbour.

Ciudadela, at the head of an inlet on the western coast, was the capital in the time of the Moors, and continued to be so during the Aragonese and Austrian rule. It was then the place of residence of the Governor, and was a flourishing and well-built town. Vessels of small draft, trading with Majorca and Barcelona, came up the inlet and supplied the island with foreign goods. The wall which encircled Ciudadela dates from the time of the Moors, to which more modern fortifications had been added. In the *plaza* was the Government House and the *Lonja*, or exchange, an ancient building raised on lofty Gothic arches. Thence a passage led to a postern and, by a long flight of stone steps, to the quay. The cathedral is in the centre of the town, and the largest religious edifice in the island, with a square tower and spire, all of freestone. It probably dates from the thirteenth century. Near the Mahon gate was a large convent of Austin friars, where there used to be public arguments on the philosophy of the schools. There was an extensive Franciscan convent, and a nunnery of Santa Clara. A fine *barranco* to the north supplied Ciudadela with fruit and vegetables.

The people of the island were well housed in solid stone buildings, the farmhouses being generally of two storeys, with the granary under the roof. The farmers have to contend against frequent and violent gales, a very stony and shallow soil, and scarcity of water. They are very laborious, and work under a system of partnership. There is an equal division of produce between landlord and tenant, the landlord finding buildings, implements, and cattle, the tenant seeds and labour. Very few landlords cultivate their own land.

The government of the island was on the model of that of Majorca, as established by En Jayme I. The Courts of Justice were removed from Ciudadela to Port Mahon by the English; otherwise no change was made in the civil government, which was left in the hands of the natives. The magistrates were called Jurats, so many in each Termino; and their duties were to impose taxes, see that the markets were properly supplied, and lay the hardships or grievances of the people before the Governor. These Jurats were chosen from all ranks. The Jurat-Major was a gentleman, his colleagues being chosen from merchants, artisans, and peasants—one from each class. They were elected for a year. The Jurats of the island, with the consent of the Governor, could call a General Council of their body, consisting of twenty-four members, which met at Ciudadela. Their business was to settle the taxes and decide upon the incidence of taxation, as well as to provide for special contingencies and to represent grievances. Besides the Jurats, there was a Bayle or Judge, who held a court and decided cases, there being an appeal to the supreme court at Port Mahon. The ecclesiastical court was held by the Vicar-General at Ciudadela. There were five parishes, and the Curas received tithes, the other clergy being supported by Masses, fees, and collections. In 1713 there were on the island 75 secular clergy, 140 friars, and 85 nuns—in all 300; a tolerably large proportion for a population of 27,000.

Under British rule there was an end to the oppression and peculation of Governors sent to the island to mend their broken fortunes; justice was properly administered, and trade flourished. The condition of the people visibly improved during Sir Robert Walpole's long peace. The island depended on foreign trade for a third of the corn that was required, and all the oil and spirits, besides other things. It was the English money circulated by the troops that preserved the islanders from bankruptcy, and indeed enabled them to live in prosperity as compared with their former lot.

The English garrison used to consist of five infantry regiments and a company of artillery, in all 2,400 effective men. They were quartered at San Felipe, Alaior, with a detachment at Fornelle, and Ciudadela, the favourite quarters. The successive Governors took an almost fatherly interest in the island, and British rule continued to be very popular.

One of the best Governors was Brigadier Kane, who was many years ruling in Minorca, and who died there. Soon after his arrival there was a great scarcity of fresh provisions: the numbers of sheep and bullocks had dwindled almost to nothing, and chickens had also become scarce. Kane set to work to remedy the evil with great energy. He procured and imported herds of cattle and flocks of sheep. He also got large supplies of poultry from France, Italy, and the Barbary coast, distributing them among the farmers and peasants; and he encouraged the people to set to work improving their breeds. Kane also made an excellent road for the whole length of the island, from Ciudadela to Port Mahon.

The British occupation was not wholly without permanent record, both as regards general history and some scientific results. Mr. John Armstrong, the Government Engineer, described the island, its physical aspects, antiquities, people, and institutions in a series of letters which were published as

'The History of the Island of Minorca' in 1752. Dr. George Cleghorn resided for many years on the island as Surgeon-Major to the garrison. In 1751 he published his 'Observations on the Epidemical Diseases in Minorca,' a work which contains a list of 180 species of plants of the island, with Latin, English, and Minorcan names.[36]

The first period of British rule lasted for nearly half a century, from 1708 to 1757, when there was a catastrophe.

CHAPTER VI
MINORCA TWICE LOST

The Seven Years' War commenced in March 1756, and the first enterprise of the French was designed against Minorca. The preparations at Toulon were, however, concealed from a dull and apathetic English Ministry by pretended activity in the ports of the Channel, to instil a belief that an invasion of England was intended. Newcastle was Prime Minister, Anson at the Admiralty, and Henry Fox Secretary of State. Pitt did not take office until the following year. The English Ministers were completely duped. Meanwhile the French had got ready thirteen sail of the line and fifteen thousand troops; and at last, when the danger of losing Minorca became apparent, hurry and confusion took the place of sloth and apathy.

Even then only ten ships were ordered to the Mediterranean, incompletely manned and without hospital or fire ships. The command was given to Admiral John Byng, fourth son of Lord Torrington, who had served under his father on board the *Superbe* at the defeat of the Spanish fleet off Cape Passaro. Byng sailed from Spithead on April 7, 1756, arriving at Gibraltar on May 2. Here he found the *Louisa*, Captain Edgcombe, who reported that he had been driven from Minorca by a French fleet of thirteen sail of the line, commanded by Admiral Galissonière, who had landed the Duc de Richelieu on the island with fifteen thousand men. Byng demanded a battalion of infantry from General Fowke, the Governor of Gibraltar, to reinforce the Minorca garrison. After consulting a council of war, this demand was refused by the Governor. There was one regiment, commanded by Lord Robert Bertie, in the fleet, and about thirty officers who had been on leave, including General Stuart, Lord Effingham, and Colonel Cornwallis, coming out to rejoin their regiments at Minorca.

While Byng was on his way, General Blakeney, the Governor of the island, was besieged by the Due de Richelieu in the castle of San Felipe. Byng sailed on May 8, and was off Majorca on the 10th, where he was joined by the *Phœnix* (Captain Hervey), who confirmed the news brought by Captain Edgcomb to Gibraltar. Byng's fleet consisted of the—

Ramillies (90)   *Kingston* (60)
Culloden (74)   *Defiance* (60)
Buckingham (68)   *Louisa* (56)
Lancaster (66)   *Portland* (48)
Trident (64)   *Deptford* (48)
Intrepid (64)   *Chesterfield* (40)

Captain (64)   *Phœnix* (22)
Revenge (64)   *Dolphin* (22)
              Experiment (22)

On the 19th the British fleet was off Port Mahon. Byng saw the Union Jack still flying on the castle of San Felipe, but several French batteries were bombarding the walls. His orders were to save Minorca at all hazards. These orders were positive and explicit, and it was his duty to carry them out at whatever sacrifice. The sight of General Blakeney still holding out and hoping for relief would have aroused the ardour of most men. The French fleet came in sight, and Byng stood towards it, making the signal for line of battle ahead at 2 P.M. The French, being about two leagues distant, tacked to gain the weather-gage, and Byng did the same. Next morning was the 20th. It was hazy in the forenoon, but at noon it cleared, and Byng made a signal to bear away two points from the wind and engage the enemy.

Rear-Admiral West, with his division, bore away seven points, and attacked the French fleet with such impetuosity that several of their ships were put out of action. The French centre kept its position, and Byng did not advance. This prevented West from following up his advantage. If the Commander-in-Chief had shown equal zeal, the French fleet would have been defeated and Minorca saved. As it was, by holding back he gave Admiral Galissonière time to retreat out of danger. The wind enabled Byng to fight if he would, when a complete victory would have been the result. But he would not.

On the absurd plea that Gibraltar might be in danger, Admiral Byng returned to that fortress, and Galissonière took up his former station off the entrance to Port Mahon. Blakeney and his gallant companions were abandoned to their fate. Nevertheless, they held out until June 28, after a brave defence of ten weeks, when the Governor surrendered to the Duc de Richelieu on very honourable terms.

Admiral Byng arrived at Gibraltar on June 19, where he found Commodore Broderick with a reinforcement of five ships of the line. The Commander-in-Chief therefore resolved to return to Minorca, and was making preparations for a second attempt. In the midst of this tardy activity the *Antelope* frigate arrived with Admirals Hawke and Saunders and Lord Tyrawly on board. Their orders were to supersede Admirals Byng and West and Governor Fowke, and to send them home under arrest. Sir Edward Hawke at once sailed for Minorca, but found the French flag flying over the castle of San Felipe. Admiral Galissonière had retired to Toulon, and there was nothing left to be done.

The people of England were furious at the loss of Minorca, venting all their rage on the unfortunate Admiral and none on the incapable Ministry which had shown apathy and want of foresight and capacity, and had neglected measures which, if taken in time, would have made Port Mahon safe from attack.

The prisoners arrived at Portsmouth in July. Admiral West was graciously received by the King and made a Lord of the Admiralty. General Fowke was dismissed the service. Byng was taken to Greenwich, where he remained a close prisoner until December. He was then brought back to Portsmouth, to be tried by court-martial. The Court sat for a month. Admiral West deposed that there was no reason why the rest of the fleet should not have engaged the enemy as closely as he did; also that there was no signal for giving chase when the enemy retreated. General Blakeney said that boats might have passed between the garrison and the fleet, and that if the troops ordered for his relief had been landed he could have held out until the arrival of Sir Edward Hawke. Captain Gardiner, of the flagship, deposed that he advised the Admiral to bear down on the enemy, but without effect, and that the Admiral took command of the *Ramillies* entirely upon himself on the day of the action. The court found that he had not done his utmost to destroy the ships of the enemy that it was his duty to engage, but that this did not proceed from want of courage or disaffection.

Lord Anson, the First Lord of the Admiralty, resigned, and was succeeded by Lord Temple, who had to discuss the sentence with George II. He drew a parallel between Byng's conduct at Minorca and George's own conduct at Oudenarde in 1708; leaving the King to draw the necessary inference that if Byng deserved to be shot, George deserved to be hanged. The King said afterwards: 'Temple is so disagreeable a fellow that there is no bearing him.' Admiral West, when he found that it was intended to shoot Byng, resigned his seat at the Admiralty. His evidence against Byng had been damning, but he would not be a party to his execution. Nor would he serve afloat under such a Ministry, saying that 'he was determined to forego anything rather than serve on terms which subject an officer to the treatment shown Admiral Byng. He was not convicted of cowardice nor of disaffection, but of misconduct, an offence never till now thought capital.' Admiral West was of opinion that the word 'negligence' in the Article of War was only intended to refer to one of those two crimes, cowardice or disaffection— 'that is, *negligence proceeding from cowardice or disaffection.*' He said that was the opinion of the House of Commons when the Bill was before them. Admiral Forbes, another Lord of the Admiralty, who held similar views, resigned at the same time.

Admiral Byng certainly deserved to be dismissed from the service; but his execution was a political murder. He was shot on March 14, 1758, after eight months of close arrest. He had forty years of naval service. George II. would show no mercy, and there was a malignant political clique whose neglect of duty would be lost sight of through this persecution of a scapegoat even unto death. The mistaken resentment of a deluded populace was stimulated to the utmost. The loss of Minorca was due quite as much to the neglect of Ministers in not taking earlier steps for its defence as to the misconduct of Admiral Byng.

At the peace in 1763 Minorca was restored to England, and enjoyed another nineteen years of good government and prosperity, making altogether sixty-seven years.

But when the American colonies broke out in rebellion and the chief Powers of Europe seized the opportunity to attack our country in its great difficulty—first France, then Spain, then Holland, England's enemies, thought their opportunity had come. They were mistaken, for England is never greater than when surrounded by enemies. She gave France her answer off Martinique; France and Spain together in Gibraltar Bay. But she could not be everywhere, and poor little Minorca was lost. While England was dealing back such telling blows elsewhere, the French and Spaniards landed, and laid siege to the castle of San Felipe. Their leader, De Crillon, pushed on the attack, but the English Governor, General Murray, made a most gallant defence. It was in 1782. Murray did not surrender until his garrison was reduced to six hundred men, while the besiegers had twelve thousand. It was typical of the whole war—England standing proudly at bay and dealing out far more than she got, with rebels, French, Spaniards, Dutch, all yelping round her. Peace was signed in 1783, but Minorca was lost.

Don Luis Berton de los Balbs, Duke of Crillon, Marquis of Valleron, and Count of St. Pol, was made a Grandee of Spain and Duke of Mahon in 1790 for subduing six hundred English soldiers by starvation with an army of twelve thousand men. He died in 1796. The second Duke of Mahon was Viceroy of Navarre for Joseph Bonaparte, and a traitor to his country. His niece Victoriana, Duchess of Mahon, succeeded to all the titles, and was living in 1870.

Thus was Minorca twice lost, after most gallant defences against tremendous odds by Generals Blakeney and Murray. The little island was destined once more to become a British possession for a few years, and then to be separated from her truest and best friends for ever.

CHAPTER VII
THE THIRD OCCUPATION OF MINORCA—
LOSS OF BRITISH RULE

When the War of the French Revolution broke out England had no base within the Mediterranean. The necessity for such a base was very much increased when Napoleon got possession of Malta. Lord St. Vincent had taken the command of the Mediterranean station in December 1795; on February 14, 1797, he fought the great battle which gave him his title, and afterwards kept up the blockade of Cadiz. He knew that Napoleon was meditating the Egyptian expedition, and detached Nelson with thirteen sail of the line to watch and, if possible, to intercept the enemy. At the same time he sent home an urgent appeal for reinforcements, and Sir Roger Curtis was sent to him with eight sail of the line.

Lord St. Vincent came to the conclusion that the possession of a base within the Mediterranean for the English fleet was of such importance that it was necessary to occupy Minorca once more. He was not a man to let the grass grow under his feet. He had no sooner come to this conclusion than he proceeded to act upon it. He organised a squadron of six ships, to be led by Commodore Duckworth:

Leviathan (74), Commodore Duckworth.
Centaur (74), Captain John Markham.
Argo (44), Captain J. Bowen.
Aurora (28), Captain Caulfield.
Cormorant (20), Captain Lord Mark Kerr.
Peterel (16), Captain Charles Long.

The squadron convoyed several transports with troops under the command of General the Hon. Charles Stuart, a younger son of the Earl of Bute, the Prime Minister. After a tedious passage, owing to contrary winds, the squadron brought to within five miles of the port of Fornelle, on the north coast of Minorca, on November 7, 1798. Fornelle is a very large and spacious harbour, but it contains many shoals and much foul ground. On the west side of the entrance there is an old fort, consisting of four bastions connected by curtains. On the other side there is an *atalaya* or signal station. After a reconnaissance, it was decided that Fornelle was not a desirable place for landing the troops. It was decided to send the smaller ships and transports to Addaya Creek, while the two line-of-battle ships stood off and on outside.

Addaya forms a large harbour on the north-east coast of the island, with a valley surrounded by lofty bare hills, which shelter it from the bleak north-westerly winds. The valley produces every kind of vegetable in abundance, while the vineyards and fruit gardens yield grapes, oranges, and pomegranates in profusion. One of the very few springs in the island sends down a stream, whence irrigating channels were conducted to every part of the valley. This is one of the most delightful spots in Minorca; but the harbour is full of rocks, and is only safe for small vessels.

Here General Stuart landed his troops and immediately occupied the surrounding heights, the Spaniards retreating to Ciudadela and Port Mahon. There was no fighting, and the whole island surrendered to General Stuart, including the castle of San Felipe, on November 15.

The Commodore, hearing a report of strange sail being in sight, proceeded to Ciudadela with the *Leviathan* and *Centaur*, and at daybreak on the 13th five sail were reported from the *Centaur's* masthead. An exciting chase was at once commenced. The strangers were large Spanish frigates, and they hauled their winds for Majorca. The *Leviathan* returned to Ciudadela that evening. Captain Markham of the *Centaur* set every stitch of canvas and continued the chase until the 14th, but he was completely outsailed by the Spaniards. He returned to Port Mahon on the day of the surrender, writing home that 'the whole island is now in our possession, without loss of any kind.' He received 884*l.* 6*s.* 8*d.* as his share of the capture of Minorca.

The possession of Port Mahon, in a war with France and Spain combined, provided a base for the fleet whence the Spanish coast could be harassed and the approaches to Toulon watched and hindered.

The *Centaur* (Captain Markham) and *Cormorant* (Captain Lord Mark Kerr) cruised along the coast of Catalonia, doing some damage to the enemy in February 1799. The ports of Cambrils and Salou, memorable as the places of embarkation of En Jayme I. and his successors, received unpleasant visits: the guns on the fort at Cambrils were dismounted, and a large Spanish frigate was driven on shore and became a wreck. The *Centaur* and *Cormorant* passed April at Port Mahon, and in May Lord Mark Kerr received orders to take home General Stuart and his staff.

In the end of the year Lord Keith had arrived with eleven ships of the line, as second in command to Lord St. Vincent, and continued the blockade of Cadiz. The Commander-in-Chief, owing to ill-health, was living on shore at Gibraltar. Suddenly the news arrived that Lord Bridport had allowed the French fleet of twenty-five sail of the line, commanded by Admiral Bruix, to give him the slip from Brest. On May 4 the French fleet came in sight of Lord Keith, who formed in line and offered battle. But a gale of wind was blowing, and Bruix bore up for the Mediterranean. Keith came to Gibraltar to report the great event to Lord St. Vincent, and the old veteran at once hoisted his flag on board the *Ville de Paris* and took command, ill as he was.

Taking Lord Keith under his orders, he proceeded with the fleet to Port Mahon, the object being to engage the enemy and prevent him from getting into Toulon.

At midnight on May 21 Lord St. Vincent made sail towards Toulon; but on June 2 he became so ill that he was obliged to return to Port Mahon, and on the 18th he resigned the command to Lord Keith and went home. On July 3 the fleet came in sight of Toulon, the *Centaur* (Captain Markham) being ahead. Owing to some news he received, Lord Keith then crowded all sail for the Bay of Rosas, in hopes of intercepting the French fleet. But there was disappointment, and once more he shaped a course for Toulon. The *Centaur* was always the advanced ship, well ahead, the frigate *Bellona* being five miles astern, and the rest of the fleet out of sight. At 9 A.M. on June 18 five strange sail were reported from the masthead. A very exciting chase immediately began at a distance of about sixty miles from Cape Sicie on the French coast. The strangers proved to be three French frigates and two brigs. After nine hours the *Centaur* came up with the sternmost frigate, and fired into her. She struck, and Captain Markham made a signal to the *Bellona* to take possession. Again making all sail, he came up first with the second and then with the third frigate, which both struck, as well as the brigs. The prizes were brought to Port Mahon, and all were taken into the British Navy.

Lord Keith cruised off Toulon for some days and then went to Genoa; but still there were no authentic tidings of the French fleet. Once more he stood towards Minorca, and received a reinforcement of twelve sail of the line under Admiral Collingwood. But on June 24 the French fleet left the Mediterranean, and on July 12 it was at Cadiz. Lord Keith determined to try for news at Gibraltar, arriving on the 14th, only to receive the maddening intelligence that the enemy was just two days ahead of him. Then began a desperate chase; for if the French fleet could be forced to give battle, it would be the most momentous event in the war. On the 30th Lord Keith left Gibraltar with thirty-one sail of the line. He was just too late. The *Centaur* looked into Brest and saw forty sail of the line safely anchored there, being the French fleet under Admiral Bruix and the Spanish fleet under Admiral Mazaredo. They had got in only six hours before, and Keith was gaining on them fast. Lord Keith, stung with anguish at the disappointment, sadly returned to Port Mahon.

Minorca continued to be a very important base for the operations of the British fleet, whence Lord Keith obtained his memorable successes on the coast of Egypt. But when the Peace of Amiens was signed on March 26, 1802, Minorca was ceded to Spain. The long connection of the little island with England was thus severed for ever, and to the Minorcans was only left a tradition and a memory of happier and more prosperous times.

Such prosperity as Minorca has since enjoyed has been due to her excellent harbour, the fame of which as a safe place of refuge gave rise to Andrea Doria's well-known proverb:

Los puertos del Mediterraneo son.
Junio, Julio, Agosto y Puerto Mahon.

So long as sailing ships were the means of locomotion at sea, crowds of merchant vessels frequented the port. It was also visited by the British fleet in the Mediterranean, which always received a cordial welcome in memory of the good old times. The Spanish Government undertook stupendous works of fortification at Cape Mola, on the eastern side of the entrance of Port Mahon. The introduction of steam reduced the importance of the harbour, which became less and less frequented. The garrison was withdrawn and the works at Cape Mola were abandoned, all sources of wealth to the islanders. Minorca has indeed fallen from its high estate. There is stagnation and poverty. A former Consul,[37] in lamenting this decadence, truly said that 'those who do visit Minorca will find a bright little town and friendly inhabitants, some of whom yet express in broken English their love for England, while they speak joyously and feelingly of the good and flourishing times when Minorca was under British rule.'

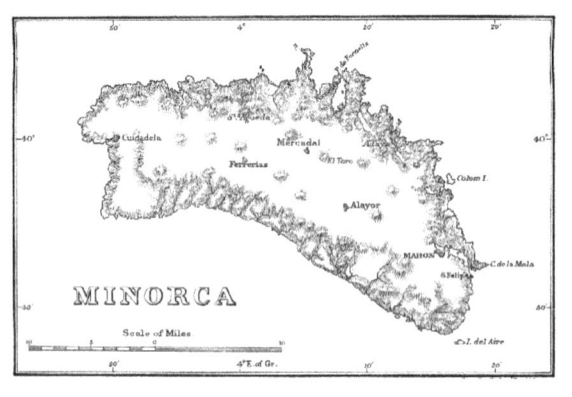

MINORCA

Milton Keynes UK
Ingram Content Group UK Ltd.
UKHW030908151124
451262UK00006B/892